HOW TO COLLEGE

A Humorous Guide To The Four Years

WRITTEN BY

BILL JEAKLE
EUGENE REARDON
ED WYATT

ILLUSTRATED BY

PHILIP CHALK

PRIMER PRESS

PALO ALTO, CALIFORNIA

BOSTON • RIO DE JANEIRO

Published by Primer Press
P.O. Box 3710
Palo Alto, California 94305

Library of Congress No: 82-099932
ISBN: 0-910617-00-7
Manufactured in the United States of America.
First printing September 1982.

10   9   8   7   6   5   4   3   2   1

Acknowledgements

Few, few preps assisted us in the preparation of this book. But the list of people who did help in some way or another is as long as that of those who refused to help. Hence our gratitude to that latter group.

Special thanks are in order for the people who backed us from the beginning: William and Elinor Reardon, Eleanor Linehan, C.T. Gleason, Matt Reardon, Neal Reardon, Edwin and Nancy Jeakle, Harold Montgomery, and Mark Allegrotti.

We are extremely grateful to those who assisted in the production of *How To College*: Karen Askey (copyediting), Fred Beltrandi (photography and English accent), Dave Wolff (graphic arts), Clark Beyer (writing and sarcasm), Dave Refuerzo (graphic arts), Warren Habib (special consultant), Grace Evans (typesetting), Brenda Jones (graphic arts), Hugh Wyatt (copyediting), and Tracy Watkins (design).

Many thanks are also owed to those who appeared in or donated photographs: Steve Zansberg, Russell Leonard, Becky Hartman, Jim Hanford, Bill Rivers, Doug Mitchell, Diva Magpayo, Ricardo Ortiz, Mark Swanson, Dave Montgomery, Jim Sandling, Dana Marie Bunnett, Tom Coffey, Shelly Finn, Bob Boutin, George Bengston, Steve Ferruolo, Andy Hargadon, Julia Wyatt, Allison Massey, Alpha Omicron Pi sorority at Duke University, Steve Swain, Kevin Kolb, Dave Henderson, Clarke Taylor, Randi Larson, Jennifer Masek, Christina Haase, Lisa Stern, Tracy Landauer, Merritt Farren, Brett Thompson, Rick Longyear, Mary Therese Kerrigan, Pat Bosque, Robert and Mary Bosque, Julia Martino, Bob Buika, Todd Graham, Karen Brower, Jackie Gonzales, Marc Shor, Stanford University Department of News and Publicity, Harvard University News Office, John Wagner, and Cohen (the dog).

Finally, we would like to thank the people who lent us their support and guidance throughout the course of this project: Patrick Reardon, Roxane Reardon, the Wyatt family, Dave Jeakle, Cathy Jeakle, Joyce Weatherford, Dan Kerrigan, and Ron Navarro.

Table Of Contents

SEVEN

Page 161

DIFFERENT STROKES

SIX

Page 145

LUST TO LOVE

EIGHT

Page 181

OVER THERE

NINE

Page 195

THE LAST ACT

Preface

So you're ready for college. How could you have ever known that the high school parties, football games, and pep rallies would come to an end, and you would enter into the new and frightening world of college parties, football games, and pep rallies? It's a terrifying thought.

In no time at all, you will have decided what college you will attend, and that decision will affect your every resume, date, and cocktail party for the rest of your life. Be careful. There's nothing worse than a boring cocktail party.

ONE

FIRST
THINGS
FIRST

THE SELECTION PROCESS

Many years ago, attending college used to be the result of a monumental decision on the part of student and family. Nowadays, however, the decision is made when the child is conceived. Still, you may want to question whether or not college is right for you. Ask yourself, "Is college right for me?" Think about it. Then answer "yes." The questioning process is over.

There is more to college than just deciding to attend. Much of senior year in high school is spent in the arduous process of applying to colleges. For most, this process will consist of choosing a few possible colleges, applying to them, waiting for a reply, and deciding among the acceptances. For some, this process will be greatly abbreviated because of low high school grades or financial restraints; these students will most likely apply to schools close to home. For others, the process will be expanded as a result of either academic or athletic prowess. Aside from these anomalies, the process is fairly straightforward.

The initial step of selecting schools can be more difficult than it first seems. Just when you decide you like one school, you may talk to someone who went there and hated it. Or just when you fall in love with the beautiful picture in the brochure of another school, your parents

**50 OF THE BEST STATE SCHOOLS
IN THE COUNTRY**

1) University of Alabama.
2) University of Alaska.
3) University of Arizona.
4) University of Arkansas.
5) University of California.
6) University of Colorado.
7) University of Connecticut.
8) University of Delaware.
9) University of Florida.
10) University of Georgia.
11) University of Hawaii.
12) University of Idaho.
13) University of Illinois.
14) Indiana University.
15) University of Iowa.
16) University of Kansas.
17) University of Kentucky.
18) Louisiana State University.
19) University of Maine.
20) University of Maryland.
21) University of Massachusetts.
22) University of Michigan.
23) University of Minnesota.
24) University of Mississippi.
25) University of Missouri.
26) University of Montana.
27) University of Nebraska.
28) University of Nevada.
29) University of New Hampshire.
30) University of New Mexico.
31) State University of New York.
32) University of North Carolina.
33) University of North Dakota.
34) Ohio State University.
35) University of Oklahoma.
36) University of Oregon.
37) Pennsylvania State University.
38) University of Rhode Island.
39) Rutgers University.
40) University of South Carolina.
41) University of South Dakota.
42) University of Tennessee.
43) University of Texas.
44) University of Utah.
45) University of Vermont.
46) University of Virginia.
47) University of Washington.
48) West Virginia University.
49) University of Wisconsin.
50) University of Wyoming.

may remind you of its exorbitant tuition. Or just when you decide to apply to USC, your Uncle Leonard (with the beachfront cottage that you've had your eye on) may remind you that he went to UCLA and strongly suggest that you consider applying to there, too.

You may enlist the help of some college catalogues or interview with alumni, but all you'll discover is that everyone thinks that his or her school is the best. If you picked at random you'd probably be happy, so don't take the decision too seriously.

Once you've somehow decided on your top choices, you'll be ready to apply. This can take some time and money if you're still dealing with five or six schools. The key to a successful application is originality. Remember that somebody has to read what you write, and chances are they don't care if you were simply vice-president of the area youth choir. Make yourself stand out. Be so good that they can't help but admit you. If you're really desperate and your credentials aren't so hot, it may help to enclose a few hundred-dollar bills.

Part of the application to college includes at least one recommendation from an instructor. *Do not use a Phys. Ed. instructor,* even if you did make the most free throws in a fitness test. The best bet is a nice, not-too-bright teacher who doesn't know you well enough to list your faults. An intelligent teacher will list your strengths, and then follow them with a "but . . . " You're trying to get into college; this isn't the time for "buts."

After applying, there's nothing to do but wait. Reach for a magazine. Or two. It might take a while.

Before you know it, you'll be admitted to one or more of the colleges of your choice (unless you didn't get in, in which case you should start stregthening your gas-pumping wrist), and then you'll be ready for the final decision. Will it be school number one? School number two? Or school number three? Or would you rather go for the curtain where Carol is standing? After getting into a few schools, it might be wise to visit them, trying to be completely objective while you're there. Of course, if you visit one school during exam week and the other during fraternity and sorority rush, it will be difficult to be objective. Do the best you can. The school that you finally pick should have the academic and social atmosphere that attracts you, a price that your family can afford, and a huge number of the opposite sex. This is the stuff that makes for a great college career.

The

First

The university began in the twelfth century as a center for educating priests and monks in non-religious matters. The earliest of these centers, Bologna and Paris, became know as Universities in the modern sense when they began to admit foreign and secular students, and when their football teams finally began to have winning seasons.

The first American institution of higher education was Harvard College, founded in 1636. Most of the early graduating classes were small (40 at Harvard in 1775), with most graduates becoming ministers, although a few went on to become insurance salesmen.

Colleges

To Each A College

Not all colleges were created equal. There is no one type of college any more than there is one type of person or lawnmower. Each college has its own character, mystique, or intrigue. The gamut of college atmospheres has several main categories, which, when understood, can make college selection a bit easier. After all, you don't want to be looking at a woman's college if you're the captain of the wrestling team.

The Traditional Christian School. Most often located in the South, this bastion of learning stresses morals, cleanliness, and early bedtime. Alcohol is not only forbidden, but the very word is frequently removed from the libraries' dictionaries. Dating becomes very structured, usually revolving around a fraternity and sorority (Greek) environment. Football is often a very popular sport, since it gives the students a chance to get out all of their pent-up aggressions.

The Woman's College. Though once thought to be an endangered species of colleges, a new wave of conservativism has made this institution popular once again. The idea of looking for a "MRS." degree at a "finishing school" still exists. Dating becomes a suitcase phenomenon with girls going to guys'

schools for weekend frat bashes. Conversely, when the guys come to the girls' school, the game of parietals (as those ancient cur-

fews are called) begins. Generally, the reward for breaking the rules isn't worth the hassle, but the feeling of accomplishment at going against the establishment can be fun.

The Intellectual School. In its brochure, this school will claim that "more true learning takes place in the lunchroom than in the classroom." Strange how class always seems to cost more than lunch. Students at this school will turn in papers on "The Metaphysical Reality of Being in the Works of Thomas Acquinas," but on Friday night they'll guzzle beer and tell dirty jokes just like other college

Photo courtesy Harvard University

students. The main difference between an intellectual school and a normal one is that at the former they keep telling you that you're smart (and pretty soon you start believing them), whereas at the latter you have to find out on your own.

The State School. People, people, and more people. Crowds at registration. Campouts at the gate for a football game. Hundreds of buildings resembling government housing - all of these scenarios are common to the state school. Since the application deadline is the latest of all schools and the tuition is cheap, you may be tempted to go here. If you do select the state school, you'll have four years of freedom before getting your degree, marrying someone you've met at a frat party, and picking up season tickets to all the games.

The Community College. This college is usually inexpensive, crowded, and pretty dull. Most often located in a bad area of town, the community college's most popular major is judo. Lack of school spirit leads to parties that are bad, at best. Most people stay close to their high school friends and meet few new people at school. The community college admits to being only an extension of high school in almost every way, except now you'll be able to cut classes and not get punished.

The Technical School. SAT scores for math range from about 780 to 800 (verbal not applicable). Social life at this school is when the Xerox man comes to sell his new line of products. They don't drink beer here, they measure and accelerate it. The students come from all over the world, but end up going to the same places: good jobs.

The College World According to Snead

When choosing a college, you must take all factors into account: reputation, number of the opposite sex, libraries, number of the opposite sex, postgraduate placement record, and number of the opposite sex. Often the best way to analyze all the factors about colleges is to purchase one of the many college guides that are available. Several of these guides exist, offering the official university view of the school, opinions of past students, or the viewpoints of learned outsiders. Probably the least popular of these guides, however, is the viewpoint of a less-than-learned outsider. *Snead's Guide to Colleges,* written by Ed Snead, a small gas station and general store owner from Arkadelphia, Arkansas, has been misguiding handfuls of students for years. Here are a few excerpts:

Princeton

Location: Back East.
Enrollment: Coupla' thousand.
Expenses: Oh, it's gotta be about ten or twelve grand.

This place is nothin' but a place where a bunch of rich snobs go live with other rich snobs and learn how to be richer snobs. I never did much care for these "intellectual" types. Probably influenced by Communists.

Notre Dame

Location: South Bend, Indiana. I got an aunt there.
Enrollment: How many do you need on a football team? About thirty or forty, I guess.
Expenses: They're all on scholarship.

Great team, except they usually have a real hard time with USC. I think they should run a passing offense more. Great school, but I think they're pretty Catholic.

University of California at Berkeley

Location: Somewhere in California, I think.
Enrollment: Must be thousands and thousands. They'll take any low-life off the street.
Expenses: I bet it's free. The only thing they have to pay for is drugs.

All they ever do at this place is burn buildings and tie up hardworking people. It's ridiculous. They go around with Communism and no morals and talk about peace and being free. Why the President doesn't have this place closed down I just don't understand. Gives the hippies a place to go.

Arkadelphia A & M

Location: Go two blocks south from my door and take a left. You can't miss it.

Enrollment: A thousand or so. My kid went there.

Expenses: Cost me a couple hundred, but it was worth it.

Best education money can buy. My kid majored in Industrial Farming and had damn good grades, too, let me tell you that. Hell of a school.

The First Look

Before you begin the actual application process, and even before you start preparing for the SAT (Scholastic Aptitude Test), you'll probably want to visit a few colleges nearby to get a feel for college campuses. By then you'll be overwhelmed with curiousity. You'll want to verify the stories you've heard from older friends: complete freedom to go and come as you please; guys and girls sharing the same bathrooms; ten-foot stereo speakers blasting the Cars out of a sixth story dorm room.

You may be able to talk Mom and Dad into taking you on a few weekend trips to distant colleges; these trips usually succeed in knocking off a day or two of school.

If you're over eager about visiting colleges, and a college turns down your request for a tour because you're fifteen, you'll have to be a little persistent. Try going back and telling them you're a French graduate student and you're very interested in their physics department because you're doing extensive research on the way atoms collide. Don't forget a heavy accent.

Photo courtesy Stanford University

Name   Address   Phone #   Sex

a b c d e f g h i j k l m n o p q r s t u v w x y z

0 1 2 3 4 5 6 7 8 9

M ○
F ○
Other ○

This Is Only A Test

Compared to a lot of things in life, such as calculus or asking someone out, the SAT is not hard. It is not, however, easy.

Preferred Wine

Chablis ○
Rose ○
Champagne ○
Other ○

Like to Dance?

Y ○
N ○

Free Sat Night?

Y ○
N ○

How About a Movie?

Y ○
N ○

The SAT

Ostensibly, the purpose of the SAT is to provide a uniform quantitative measure to compare the abilities of students applying to college, but for many, the SAT is just a cause for anxiety. In fact, it is the third leading cause of death among teenagers, behind pimples and listening to AM radio.

Some progressive high schools provide classes to help prepare for this dreaded test. Courses such as "Word Power" or "How to Cheat on the SAT" have noticeably improved students' scores. Most of these classes provide sample SAT questions so that the student can get an idea of how the test will be run.

MATH and ENGLISH

1) Given circle O and points G and D. If OD = OG = GD, does GOD exist?

a) Yes
b) No
c) In an irrational universe, how can we be sure?
d) Yeah, and boy is he mad!
e) What?

2) In the figure shown, circle O has a radius of 10 pi. If the perimeter of EFGH is 13 12/17, then who played short for the Yankees in the '61 World Series?

a) 13 12/17
b) 17 12/13
c) 12 17/13
d) Tony Kubek
e) 13 13/13

Grammar. Choose the best answer for the capitalized part.

2) The milkman, rarely bringing milk with him, came to Mrs. Jones' house at 8:00 a.m. daily to deceive Mr. Jones, until one day THEY WERE SEEN BY HIM.

    a) No change
    b) Mr. Jones shot him.
    c) Mr. Jones joined in.
    d) The Mormon Tabernacle choir was under the bed.
    e) They ran out of Jello.

Reading Comprehension. Read the following passage and then answer the questions.

3) Buffy's mother gave her two dollars to buy a loaf of bread and some milk at the store. On the way, Buffy ran into a man who was selling pork belly futures. The man told Buffy, "It's as good an investment as buying GM short and the dividend outlay is twice the capital gains in half the grace period." Buffy was convinced and invested a dollar of her mother's money. Before going to the store, Buffy promised the man she would return soon to see how the investment was doing. At the store, Buffy realized that she did not have enough money for both bread and milk, so she bought Screaming Yellow Zonkers instead. On her way back, she saw the man, who told her that the investment had earned her $2,678,498.23 in the market. Buffy decided to sell, move to the Riviera, and marry a wealthy jet-setter.

The theme of this story is:

    a) Success.
    b) Good thing Buffy wasn't Jewish.
    c) Bread and milk do not a multimillionaire make.
    d) Bland and vapid. The story is saved only by its repartee and sense of timing, delicately balanced with its complex character sketches which more than adequately outline the futility of life as a result of woman's struggle against man and a male-oriented society, while adding a cosmic sense and a universal backdrop.
    e) Screaming Yellow Zonkers cost less than one dollar.

The Ins And Outs Of Applying

One day you'll come home from school, throw down your coat and begin to relax over a bowl of Captain Crunch when Mom will ask if anyone has brought in the mail. In passive response, you'll pull your sights from the T.V. and reply that you'll get it. The trek out to the mailbox will be a casual stroll,

The Ins

Acceptances and rejections come in all forms. Contained in the midst of your thick envelope will be the acceptance letter. If you've applied to a normal school, the letter should look like the one below. If you've applied to a special school, you'll receive a special letter of acceptance; these are presented also.

Normal School

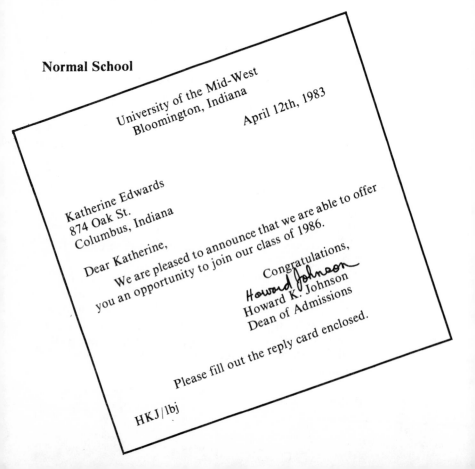

University of the Mid-West
Bloomington, Indiana

April 12th, 1983

Katherine Edwards
874 Oak St.
Columbus, Indiana

Dear Katherine,

We are pleased to announce that we are able to offer you an opportunity to join our class of 1986.

Congratulations,

Howard Johnson
Howard K. Johnson
Dean of Admissions

Please fill out the reply card enclosed.

HKJ/lbj

and the day will seem like any other in spring.

Flipping through the mail, you'll routinely check to see if there's anything for you. Suddenly, a letter from one of the universities will confront you. You'll start to think,"What a hassle, somebody lost my application." Then it will occur to you that it's not a postcard, but a real letter. Panic will set in. You won't want to open it. First, you'll take a deep breath of fresh air; then you'll savagely tear the envelope and Fate will

Formal School

The Academy of Our Lady of the Holy Sciences
16531 Ostentatiousness Boulevard
Village of Academia, Swarthington, Pennsylvania

The Sixth of the Month of April
Nineteen-Hundred Eighty-Three

Jonathan Livingston Seagull
12645 Espadrille Promenade
The City of Saint Louis
Missouri

Our Dearest Admitted & Newest Member,

It is to be hereby known that the aforementioned recipient of this notice of self-evident truth has been heretofore selected to enter the world of academia with our beloved university if he or she so desires.

The Academy of Our Lady of the Holy Sciences would most heartily like to congratulate our young warriors of learning and knowledge on their past and present achievements.

With Warmest and Deepest Sincerity,

The Committee for the Determination of Acceptees and Rejectees Based on the Performances of the Aforesaid Persons

Please fill out the reply card enclosed.

cc: 1453 Other Newest and Dearest Members

come pouring out into your hands.

Thick envelope? Good sign. Start blowing off the rest of senior year. Thin envelope? Let's face it. This college is on the decline and has a very unrealistic guy/girl ratio, anyway. Start cursing yourself for ever applying there in the first place.

Informal School

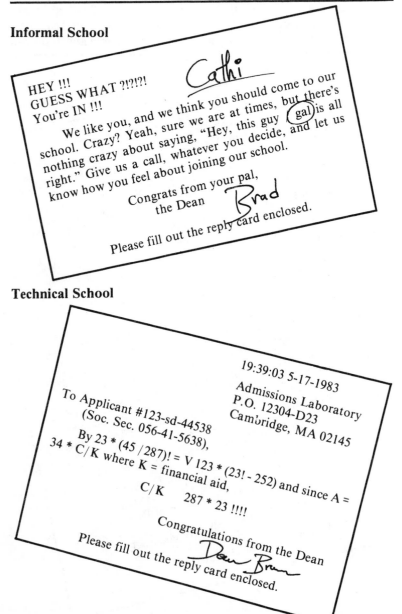

HEY !!! GUESS WHAT ?!?!?! You're IN !!!

Cathi

We like you, and we think you should come to our school. Crazy? Yeah, sure we are at times, but there's nothing crazy about saying, "Hey, this guy (gal) is all right." Give us a call, whatever you decide, and let us know how you feel about joining our school.

Congrats from your pal,
the Dean   Brad

Please fill out the reply card enclosed.

Technical School

19:39:03 5-17-1983

Admissions Laboratory
P.O. 12304-D23
Cambridge, MA 02145

To Applicant #123-sd-44538
(Soc. Sec. 056-41-5638),

By 23 * (45/287)! = V 123 * (23! - 252) and since A =
34 * C/K where K = financial aid,

C/K   287 * 23 !!!!

Congratulations from the Dean   Dan Brun

Please fill out the reply card enclosed.

The Outs

Obviously, you won't want to receive bad news of any form, and rejection notices do not warm the heart no matter how they're written. Most colleges really try to make you feel better when you receive the bad news. Other schools don't; they prefer to write simpler rejections.

Rejection Letter

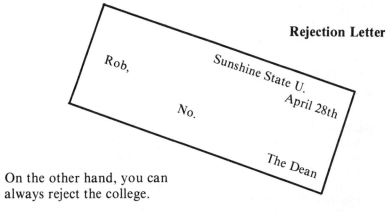

Rob,

Sunshine State U.

April 28th

No.

The Dean

On the other hand, you can always reject the college.

Rejection Letter II

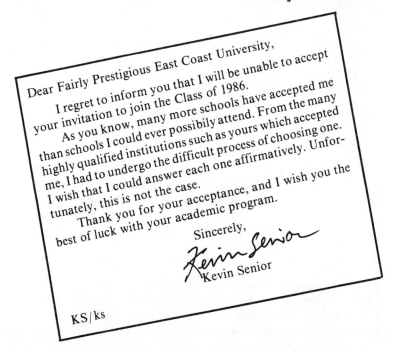

Dear Fairly Prestigious East Coast University,

I regret to inform you that I will be unable to accept your invitation to join the Class of 1986.

As you know, many more schools have accepted me than schools I could ever possibily attend. From the many highly qualified institutions such as yours which accepted me, I had to undergo the difficult process of choosing one. I wish that I could answer each one affirmatively. Unfortunately, this is not the case.

Thank you for your acceptance, and I wish you the best of luck with your academic program.

Sincerely,

Kevin Senior

KS/ks

The Bucks Start Here

If you have been outstanding in academics, athletics, or some other field, you may be lucky enough to qualify for a scholarship. Scholarships are given by the colleges themselves, by the National Merit Foundation, by private companies, and by dozens of other organizations. Some of these scholarships are well-known, while others are rarely awarded due to circumstances surrounding them. Most of you will not be eligible to receive the awards listed below.

National Merit Scholarship. Awards ranging from $1,000 to $5,000 for those who have excelled in the National Merit Program.

Augustus M. Finney Liberal Arts Endowment Award. An extremely obscure scholarship given to extremely obscure people for extremely obscure reasons. Upon his death in 1918, Augustus M. Finney, the noted humanitarian and shampooist, left over $1,000,000 for "educating left-handed obese people about the danger of bathing with porpoises." This scholarship is seldom awarded.

Bob's Scholarship. Covering half tuition at Bob's College, this is given to the winner of Bob's Scholarship Lottery (tickets available at any Bob's outlet). Also includes free spaghetti dinner at Bob's Diner.

Herbert Hoover Memorial Scholarship. Given each year to the person most likely to lead the country into the worst economic depression ever known.

Daring Things To Do
Before Going To College

1) Be an A.F.S. student to Mississippi.
2) Use a #3 pencil on the SAT.
3) Include a nude picture of yourself on your college application.
4) Write a bad check to cover the application fee.
5) Turn down a full tuition scholarship to an ivy league school.
6) Request a roommate with psychological problems.

TWO

SETTLING IN

ADAPTING TO THE COLLEGE ENVIRONMENT

College begins when you are pulled from the safe womb of high school and thrust into the turbulent quagmire of the university. Security is replaced by competition, long time friends are replaced by new acquaintances, and quiet evenings in front of the TV at home are replaced by loud nights in front of the keg. As the admissions packet said, part of the magic of college is learning how to get along with all types of people, how to shun injustice, and how to do your own laundry.

In college living situations there must be a sense of equality and community. You and the other students will be using the same facilities and therefore will have to respect each other, regardless of race, creed, wealth, or opinion of Kenny Rogers. When you drop your bags down at your first college dormitory, you may wonder how you'll ever learn to be friends with the students there. You have nothing in common with them now, but it won't be long before you have everything in common with them. You'll eat with them, talk with them, drink with them, listen to music with them, laugh with them, cry with them, even sleep through classes with them. Though you and your roommate may not get along at first - one of you may be religious and studious, the other hedonistic and apathetic - the concept of student housing requires that you remain together and work things out. By the end of the year the hedonistic one will probably have become pre-med, while the studier will have taken to drugs and the Grateful Dead.

By the time you go home for the summer you'll be a changed person with new friends, a new vocabulary, and a whole new lifestyle.

The Big Day

Arrival at college is a momentous occasion. It marks the end of complete supervision by parents and the beginning of independence. Your parents may be there for a day or so to help you make the transition. They'll help you with your luggage ("Grab that trunk, dear; I'll get this poster"), suggest ways to help you decorate your room ("How about this pennant, son?"), and speak to the administrators who will be standing around ("We honestly believe the real purpose of education is to teach. We really do.")

Before your know it, though, they'll be gone, and it will just be you and a multitude of other college freshmen saying to yourselves, "Now what?" To help you answer this question, many universities have implemented a practice known as "orientation" which is designed to remove you from one lifestyle and thrust you into another as painlessly as possible. During orientation you'll begin to feel the "college experience."

Those Embarrassing Moments

If you arrive at college with your parents, you must be prepared to have them ask embarrassing questions or make embarrassing comments as you unpack. There's really no way to avoid this uncomfortable situation, but do your best to make sure your folks don't say anything too offensive.

"Wait, Rocky. Don't you want your favorite teddy bear?"

"Melissa! You didn't tell us you were going to be living with *men*."

"Remember to brush your teeth every day."

"This is what? A Chicano theme dorm? Well, if we had known that . . . "

"Your roommate's name is Mohammed? Oh, dear, that's too bad. Well, don't worry, things will work out. I'm sure you won't have any problems, Sahib."

Orientation schedules are often very ambitious.

8:00 AM: Breakfast in the cafeteria.

8:15 AM-12:30 PM: Language and math placement tests.

12:45-1:00 PM: Free time (although it is suggested that discussions of the role of the university in society take place).

1:00-3:00 PM: Campus tours given by large frat guys for girls only. All others are encouraged to spend the time looking up the word "libido."

3:00-5:00 PM: Lectures by faculty members. Choose your own topic.

"God vs. Bob Barker" Professor Stuart, room 49b.

"The Cuisinart and Its Place in Society"
Prof. Culinary, room 69.

"Those Zany Philosophers"
Prof. Marx, Confucius room.

"The Pre-med Major, or How to Cope With Pain"
Prof. Stitch, room 23c.

"The English Major, or How to Cope With Starvation"
Dr. Jones, Smith room.

"The Alphabet" (recommended for athletes)
Coach Johnson, gym.

5:00-5:15: Dinner.

5:15-6:00 PM: Free time (although it is suggested that students break into small groups with one group solving the world hunger problem, the next group working on a peaceable solution to the Middle East problem, and so on).

6:00-8:00 PM: Speech by the president of the university. Last chance to see him or hear him speak in person until graduation.

8:00-9:00 PM: Reception (although no one is sure who it is for).

9:00 PM-12:00 AM: Time when everyone stands around asking questions like "Where are you from?", "What are you going to major in?" and "What were your SAT scores?" while holding onto cups filled with beer and being drowned out by loud music. The purpose of this is to allow people to get sick and forget everyone's name as quickly as possible.

Signing In and Paying Up

Registration is the process by which you choose classes and pay bills. It can be confusing, but a few simple reminders should make the process go smoothly.

Selecting Classes. Don't think that you can't get the classes you want just because they're almost always filled by the time you register. Colleges always make classes seem full just to see how persistent you are. Use your imagination.

1) While thousands of people are crowded around the sign-up sheets, point up in the air and say, "Wow! Look at that plane!" When heads start to turn, sneak in and sign up.

2) Engineer a media blitz announcing that registration, usually held in the gym, will be in the library this year. Not only will you be alone at registration, but the rest of the student body will be suspended for making a commotion in the library, and you'll become the best student on campus.

3) Threaten a hunger strike if you don't get your classes. If nothing else, it will cut down on your food costs.

Paying. The check that you write to pay for your first term will probably be the largest you have ever written. Though many people receive some type of financial aid or loan, you should not forget how much a college education costs. Your college, however, may have one of the "bonus attractions" that are being implemented by many schools to make the financial crunch less pronounced.

1) *Breakfast in bed on day of payment* (St. Loyola Hardcourt). Why should you have to stand in line to pay thousands of dollars? The progressive St. Loyola Hardcourt College in St. Louis has solved this problem by offering breakfast in bed (omelette, danish, orange juice, coffee, champagne, and choice of hash browns or toast) for any full-paying student.

2) *Conditional payment* (North Alabama Institute of Technology). Administrators at NAIT have introduced the "conditional payment" plan. The student pays only if he or she enjoyed the class and is satisfied with the grade received. For obvious reasons, GPA's at this school are very high.

Photo courtesy Stanford University

Cash or Charge?

Eventually, you will have to cough up the money necessary for tuition, room and board, and assorted fees. When it comes to payment, you have several options.

Cash. Probably the easiest way to pay, and with the least amount of paperwork. It is a bit gauche, though; carrying a wad of hundred-dollar bills makes you look like a senior citizen who just struck it rich in Vegas.

Check. Also easy, but with serious mental repercussions. It can be a real shock when you write a check with the word "thousand" on it. In addition, you need to have two id's.

Credit Card. Just say "charge it, please", and the cost of a college education will appear on your parents' monthly bill, right between the new kitchen knives and the Scott's Turf Builder.

Deferment. At first, this may seem appealing, but beware. By the end of the term when payment is due, you'd better not have spent the tuition money on records or pizza. Unless your future lies in a record shop or a pizza parlor.

Decorating Your Room

To make your room seem more friendly and more comforting, you'll probably want to decorate it. Plants, posters, and photographs can do wonders for a previously barren dorm room. Make sure you bring or buy things which will make you feel at home in a new environment and still remain fairly tasteful. When it comes to interior decorating, take a look at these samples from last year's freshman at State U.

Hugh

Billy

Jean-Paul

John

Ex Libris

Roommate situations can sometimes be touchy. If you find yourself in one of these situations, your best bet may be to take out a lot of reading and find out what others did.

Paul Newman was my Freshman Roommate
by Becky Olson

An innocent girl from South Dakota finds her first year at a large university much more exciting than she'd ever dreamed and tells all.

Oh, Wow, Man!
by Dan Baker

Guess what happens when two California beach types are assigned as roommates, right next door to some hot chicks! Oh, wow, man! A bitchin' story with some gnarly surfing jargon and some hot jacuzzi scenes.

O.T.: The Out-Of-Towner
by Steven Gameberg

Eerie, yet heartwarming story of a young man at a huge state university who befriends roommate, a student from out-of-town who has been left behind by his parents. Soon to be a motion picture.

Getting Board

It came from the cafeteria disguised as food. Thousands of students were forced to eat it. It was . . . a University Food Service Meal! ! !

There aren't any horror movies about dorm food, but perhaps there should be. A few months in the school cafeteria may leave you wondering whether you're part of a psychology experiment or just being tortured.

All right, things aren't that bad. Aside from stretching the starchy foods a bit, most meals are edible and even tasty. Well, edible.

One positive note: since the ingredients for all the meals are roughly the same, the campus cafeteria usually becomes a haven of imagination as the cooks try to give the same old stuff some new twists.

FOOD SERVICE MENU for the Week of Oct. 25-31

	Sunday	Monday	Tuesday	Wednesday
L U N C H		Roast Beef Sandwiches French Fries Dessert de la Pomme	Beef Stew Mashed Potatoes Applesauce	Beef Casserole Mashed Potatoes Apple Cider
D I N N E R	Roast Beef au Jus Baked Potato Apple Pie a la Mode	Beef Steaklets Boiled Potatoes Candied Apples	Beef Souffle Mashed Potatoes Fruit Cup	Creamed Chipped Beef Mashed Potatoes Steamed Apples Joe's Style

SCAMMER'S MEAL PLAN

	Sunday	Monday	Tuesday
	Brunch:	Breakfast:	Sleep Late
EARLY	Slip through the cafeteria line.	Bring dirty dish to cafeteria and pretend to be going up for seconds.	Lunch:
	Dinner:		Offer to eat fast-food restaurant rejects (cold burgers, returned fries).
	Use fake meal card or doctored card from last semester.	Snack:	
		Mingle at faculty-student sherry hour.	Big Night Out:
LATE	Midnight Snack:	Dinner:	Dine'n'dash local steak house.
	Slugs into the vending machine.	Attend IBM reception for engineering students.	

Scammer's Meal Plan

All students will probably find the cost of college meal plans astronomical. Most will accept this as an unavoidable aspect of university living. Others will not. These rebels are known as "scammers," and they are so loath to buying a standard food service meal plan that they devise their own. With a little effort and imagination, costly, boring meals can be transformed into inexpensive, adventurous means of nourishment.

THE STANFORD DAILY

Press). Newcomers are especially wel come.

Wine and Cheese Hour At Professor Pootkins's home. A discussion of me- dieval literature followed by a wine and cheese get-together. Non-alcoholic drinks will be served.

General

SCIRE Credit Proposal Deadlines Stu- dents interested in designing their own project or internship for Fall come by the SCIRE Union .

Thursday	Friday	Saturday	Sunday Morn
Chipped Beef	Mystery Meat	Halloween Party!!	Note: Joe won't be in Sunday morn; fix your own vittles.
Refried Potato Mexicano	Stewed Potatoes a la Joe		
Apple Casserole	Old, Rotten Apples a la Barrel Bottom	Joe's Famous Beef Snacks	
Sloppy Joes		Homemade Potato Chips	
Sauteed Potatoes	Mystery Meat Surprise	Bobbing for Apples	
Apple Souffle	Mystery Veg Mystery Fruit		

Wednesday	Thursday	Friday	Saturday
Breakfast:	Sleep late	Late Breakfast:	Brunch:
Persuade roommate to take job at Mac's; feast on Egg McMuffins.	Big Lunch: Dress up as cafeteria worker and cart away soup and salad.	Bloat stomach and pose as poster child in front of local Unicef chapter.	Peruse newspaper for wedding or Bar Mitzvah.
Light Lunch:		(Blow off Lunch)	Smorgasbord:
Eat friend's fries while conversing over lunch.	Light Dinner: Call everyone you know; hint about being invited to dinner.	Dinner: Wearing white lab coat, introduce yourself to the cafeteria staff as the new manager; feed all your friends.	Flag down the commissary delivery truck; tell driver the storeroom has been temporarily moved to your dorm room.
Late Dinner Snack: Hold on until study break (following house meeting).			

Late Night Munchies

Everybody knows that a pop-corn popper is an essential for a college dorm room, but few are aware of the range of modern poppers available on the market.

You can always settle for the standard bucket type, but why not wow the kids with your new Poppin' Pope?

AM-FM Clock/Radio/Popper. Features both a close'n'pop top and a "wake to tasty kernels" setting that revolutionizes early morning rising. Comes in pink, green, and oxford pin-stripe. Guaranteed to raise popularity and GPA.

The "Kernel." Particulary popular with ROTC types. Comes in strategic khaki or fatigue gray.

"Poppin' Pope." At the moment of papal truth, the inspired pontiff emerges from his apartment as the buttery treats crowd into the "plaza."

Capitol Popper. Cute. Kernels go in front door to "convene." When the popping appears in the dome, an indicator flashes "heated session." "Adjourn" signals ready to serve. Best taken with a grain of salt.

Food Fads And Faves

His

1) **Haagen-Dazs Ice Cream.** Extremely popular despite the fictitious name and the fact that it's manufactured in New Jersey, not Scandinavia.

2) **Domino's Pizza.** This late-night pizza delivery firm now has branches throughout the country. A large pepperoni can make any all-nighter into a social occasion.

3) **Diet Soft Drinks.** Forget the saccharin controversy; these drinks are the light beers of the non-alcoholic world. A big favorite with college women.

4) **"Gourmet" Jelly Beans.** One of this year's most popular food fads. There must be some connection between their popularity both on campus and in the Oval Office.

5) **"Fro Yo"(Frozen Yogurt).** Fave college dessert par excellance. No one cares whether or not it's low fat, since it tastes so good.

Hers

Fun and Games

Freshmen need an outlet for the excitement of the first few weeks of school; pranks provide this outlet. Frats also enjoy pranks. Remember that freshman pranks are "good fun," frat pranks "in poor taste," and all others non-existent.

Tossing water balloons. This perennial favorite always succeeds if a dorm war is declared.
Good targets: room interiors, people, T-shirts on female torsos.
Bad targets: the Dean of Student Affairs, football players.
Alternative prank: tossing water prophylactics.

Pillow fight-attack. Use your roommate's pillow to keep your own pillow intact.

Panty raid. Could get out of hand! (see insert)

Short sheeting. To the victim, very funny, for about a minute.

Saran wrap over toilet seat. Don't get caught; you'll be hated for this one.

Streaking. Extinct.

Streaking dinosaurs. Very extinct.

Mooning a nearby dorm. Call up a South Korean businessman and ask him to guest lecture at a rival dorm.

Stealing college-named street signs. Put these on your wall to help direct traffic into and out of your room.

Things Your Parents Did at College (That You Will Never Do)

1. Knew all of the words to the school song.
2. Wore long coats to football games.
3. Went to the malt shop.
4. Majored in home economics.
5. Ignored homosexuality.
6. Played bridge.

Things You'll Do at College (That Your Parents Never Did)

1. Know all the words to Fleetwood Mac's *Rumours*.
2. Wear tuxs to McDonalds.
3. Go to the red light district.
4. Major in communications.
5. Ignore authority.
6. Have sex.

CAUTION:
Prank gone out of bounds

Guys: Sneak into girls' rooms; steal assorted underwear; toss around lounge.

Girls: Sneak into guys' rooms; steal assorted underwear; rip to shreds.

Guys: Sneak into girls' rooms; dump all contents of bureau drawers on floor; toss several evening gowns out window.

Girls: Sneak into guys' rooms; overturn all furniture; pile clothes in center of lounge; have bonfire.

Guys: Sneak into girls' rooms; smash all windows; break all furniture; destroy mattresses; burn books.

Girls: Sneak into guys' rooms; spray with machine-gun fire.

Guys: Toss hand grenades through smashed windows of girls' rooms.

Girls: Detonate small nuclear weapons in each of guys' rooms; avoid subsequent mushroom clouds.

Clothes-Minded

College dress differs considerably from that of the "real world." In fact, most non-collegiates usually express shock or disgust at campus fashions. What do those people know about style, anyway? You're in college, and you know what's right. School dress differs considerably from state to state and from school to school, but some generalizations can still be made about what is "in" and what is "out" among the university crowd.

Fashionable

Vuarnet or Ray-Ban sunglasses. Despite skimping on meals, books, and other necessities, it is imperative to spend between $40-70 on a pair of sunglasses. Why? Simple. Everyone else does.

Polo line. The Polo pony is gradually causing the alligator to go the way of the penguin. With so many bright colors, the Polo line of clothing can provide you with a new outfit for every day of the month for the rest of your life.

Bermuda shorts. The latest rage among college students. The most fashionable tend to be the longest and the loudest. Go into your attic and take an old pair from your father. Never

mind that they make you look like your neighbor when he mows the lawn; they're in.

Topsiders. It used to be that only sailors from New England

Where to Find Fashionable Clothing

Bermuda Shorts
Your house
Goodwill
Sears

Polo Clothing
Expensive department stores
Expensive department stores
Expensive department stores

Topsiders / Espadrilles
Expensive department stores
L.L. Bean
Your roommate's closet

Army Surplus Clothing
Army/Navy stores
Military bases
The Middle East

wore these, but now the whole world has them. They're even popular in Oklahoma, where the only water comes from the kitchen faucet.

Espadrilles. Cute, dressy, and they come in a million colors, so what could be better for the fashion-conscious college woman? Four years of wearing these in college will be adequate preparation for later use at cocktail parties and country club dances.

Preppy clothing. Thanks to a recent fad, the entire college clothing scene has been inundated with the "preppy look." As a result, students of all sexes, races, creeds, and economic backgrounds can be seen in khakis (skirts, slacks, and shorts), Oxford candy-striped shirts, and anything with an alligator on it. Incidentally, the rest of the world correctly identifies the animal on Lacoste apparel as a "crocodile," but since America has the highest GNP, it can call little emblems whatever it wants.

Painters' hats. No one really knows why these caught on, but the best guess is that they're inexpensive. These are especially fashionable when they include a clever slogan about an upcoming game ("Trojans pop under pressure"), but make no fashion statement at all if they are actually from a paint store and say "Joe's Paints."

T-shirts from another school. Never own more than one or two T-shirts from your own college. Instead, load up on the gear from other schools. Really fashionable: schools from opposite part of the country, schools with funny names, European schools.

Rugby Shirts. These were invented for wear at college. Never mind that few people know anything about the sport itself. *Fashion tip:* wide stripes are "in"; pack away those old rugby shirts with the thin stripes.

Army surplus clothing. Don't ask why it's fashionable for pacificistic college kids to dress up in hand-me-downs from GI's. Students probably forget that the person who previously wore the clothes was probably your basic high school loser who couldn't even get into college.

Obscure tennis shoes. Colleges, and particularly those in the sun belt, are havens for every brand of tennis shoe in the world. You'll look like a real tennis pro if you wear a pair of hard-to-find shoes. Try K-Swiss, Bata, or Diadora.

ALSO . . .

High school warmups. Great conversation starters, especially if your high school had tacky nickname like the Golden Frogs or the Jumping Gophers. Garner extra points by wearing warmups from a team of the opposite sex.

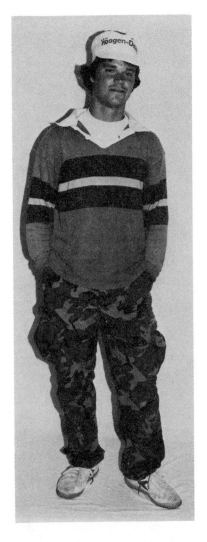

On the Border:
YES AND NO

Cowboy boots. "In" with backwoods types, Texans, and Easterners who want people to think they're rugged adventurers. "Out" with preppies, earthy types, and businessmen.

Painters' pants. Though universally accepted, these have become passe at really fashion-conscious schools.

"New Wave"/"Punk" look (thin ties, bandanas, miniskirts, leather). Accepted at liberal schools; a fad at fashion-conscious schools; not accepted at backwoods schools . . . in fact, might get you killed.

Bare feet. De rigueur at mellow, earthy schools. Not too popular at urban campuses, or in cold climates.

Not Fashionable

Polyester. Recognized in forty-nine states and Canada as a symbol of tackiness. Only acceptable if you are an alumnus, or live in Iowa.

Cut-off jeans. These will label you as either a former flower child or a "black socks on the tennis court" type.

Career clothing (three-piece suits, wing tips). Maybe as a senior. Otherwise, it makes you looks like you actually care about your future, and that's not fashionable in a place where the only thing you look forward to is the next brew.

Socks (with Topsiders). Simply not necessary.

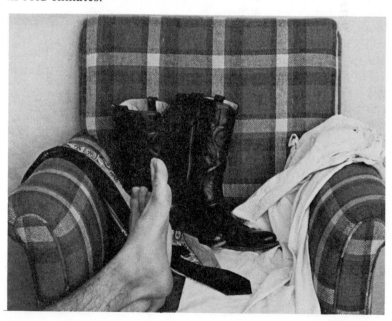

The Beat Goes On

"If music be the food of love, then play on."

Shakespeare probably didn't have college in mind when he wrote that line from *Twelfth Night*, but it is certainly applicable to many facets of collegiate music. Music, like any other fine art, is so subjective that one cannot generalize. Nonetheless, it is an essential part of college life, and don't kid yourself into thinking that you'll somehow escape its grasp. You can avoid every party on campus, miss every concert ever held, blow off every football game your school plays, and lock yourself in your room, only to have your next door neighbor put AC/DC on his $5000 stereo system and crank it up louder than a jackhammer. You've got to face facts; you'd better learn to like, or at least tolerate, some different styles of music in order to have a good time at college.

Classical

Who to talk about: Bach, Bartok, Mozart.
Who NOT to talk about: AC/DC, Led Zeppelin, Van Halen.
What to say: "The San Francisco Symphony just butchered Mozart's 41st last night. God, they need Ozawa."
What NOT to say: "It's good music, but why aren't there any words?"
How to dress for concert: Well.

Hard Rock

Who to talk about: AC/DC, Led Zeppelin, Van Halen.
Who NOT to talk about: Bach, Bartok, Mozart, the San Francisco Symphony.
What to say: "That drum solo was awesome. This is excellent."
What NOT to say: "Is this Barry Manilow?"
How to dress for concert: Badly.

Funk

Who to talk about: Rick James, P-Funk, Prince.
Who NOT to talk about: the San Francisco Symphony, Barry Manilow.
What to say: "Get down, funk it up, get down, funk it up."
What NOT to say: "Aren't the lyrics a bit repetitive?"
How to dress for concert: With portable cassette player on shoulder.

Folk Rock

Who to talk about: Dan Fogelberg, Joni Mitchell, James Taylor.
Who NOT to talk about: Rick James, AC/DC, the Pretenders.
What to say: "Let's kick back and pretend we're on the beach."
What NOT to say: "Let's crank it up and pretend we're in Jersey City."
How to dress for concert: Anything mellow is definitely cool.

A Brief History of Portable Music in College

1344: Students at the Sigma Chi fraternity at the University of Paris make fun of minstrels passing outside their window.

1567: Work study program at University of Wittenberg offers the job of troubador for the first time. Thousands apply.

1789: Henry Lee brings a harpsichord to a Harvard freshman orientation party and plays his loudest stuff while frosh stand around keg.

1867: Thomas Edison invents the phonograph and takes it to his son, who quickly becomes most popular kid in his dorm.

1935: Need for smaller portable phonographic machinery develops when students tire of lugging large Victrola and small white dog around campus.

1957: Robbie Harrison rips juke box out of the wall of Al's Campus Malt Shoppe when he runs out of quarters.

1966: The transistor radio livens up college beach parties and allows more room in back seats of cars.

1979: Birth of a two-headed child in Osaka, Japan, gives manufacturers the idea of the "box," thus revolutionizing music by making stereo portable.

1982: The Walkman replaces conversation as the college students' principal method of communication.

The Sounds Of Music

BONUS!!!
Includes the Reagan-Begin duet Mideast Magic

Selected Cuts
SOCIAL (IN)SECURITY
OLD PEOPLE'S BLUES
MY WAY
BUDGET CUT BOOGIE

The Reaganomics: NO FUTURE
(Hardline Records AC 666)

ABSOLUTELY FREE!!
Disco Version of I, Me, Mine

Selected Cuts
DRESSED FOR
SUCCESS
CAPITOL HILL
SHUFFLE
LEAVIN' ON THAT
MIDNIGHT TRAIN TO
LAW SCHOOL

Student Government: ONE FOR
THE RESUME
(Self-Centered Records ME 800)

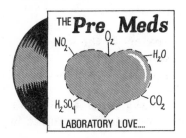

ACT NOW!
and receive FREE hit single
I Would Do Anything (to get into med school)

Selected Cuts
DISSECT THE CAT (not our love)
GRADE IT UP ALL NIGHT
MCAT MADNESS

Pre-Meds: LABORATORY LOVE
(Cutthroat Records AA 111)

Cliff Notes & The English Majors:
LET'S GET PRETENTIOUS
(Unemployed Records NO 000)

Selected Cuts
WHAT IS LIFE?
MIND GAMES
SUBJECTIVE REALITY
REAL SUBJECTIVITY

Records
College Favorites

1) *Abbey Road*, The Beatles
2) *Aja*, Steely Dan
3) *American Beauty*, The Grateful Dead
4) *Animal House Soundtrack*, Various
5) *Born to Run*, Bruce Springsteen
6) *Dark Side of the Moon*, Pink Floyd
7) *Greatest Hits*, James Taylor
8) *No Future*, The Reagonomics
9) *Songs in the Key of Life*, Stevie Wonder.
10) *Who's Next*, The Who

Party Time
Saturday Night

"Crank" these.

1) *The B-52's*, The B-52's
2) *Street Songs*, Rick James
3) *Tattoo You*, The Rolling Stones
4) *Infinity*, Journey
5) *Look Sharp!* Joe Jackson

Mellow Time
Sunday Morning

"Spin" these.

1) *Netherlands*, Dan Fogelberg
2) *Bustin' Out*, Pure Prairie League
3) *Greatest Hits*, The Spinners
4) *Revolver*, The Beatles
5) *Hasten Down The Wind*, Linda Ronstadt

Three Minutes A Day To A Stronger College Vocab

Lost at dinner conversations? Unable to follow stairway discussions? Tired of being left out? Perhaps you're on drugs. Or worse. Maybe you're suffering from new vocabulary deficiency. It's quite possible. Let's look . . .

Many college students have complained of a loss from words, of being unable to express themselves, and of being surrounded by seemingly undiscernible speech. These problems may be due to an unfamiliarity with such words as "primo," "awesome," or "L.L.Bean's." This year why not join the thousands determined to increase their mode of communication through this simple minutes-a-day course which allows you to learn new words at your own pace and comfort? Every morning you'll get psyched while learning mega amounts of words. In fact, you are already learning right now even if you didn't know it. We've underlined new vocab words in this paragraph so you can go for it and start learning in a big way.

Try indentifying a few words. If you're really keyed and you find yourself up for it, you won't bag it. Are you there?

1) Lynn is really let down about the last problem set. She expected a higher grade than usual because she worked extra hard, but to no avail. She received the same score as on the last three. She is really

    a) bummed.
    b) go for it.
    c) Margaret Thatcher.

2) Jay was outrageously excited about the upcoming game. His two favorite teams were about to rival it out, and he had just discovered that a friend could get him tickets for the game. He was

    a) happy.
    b) glad.
    c) psyched to the max.

3) At a recent house meeting, the dorm president proposes to spend house funds on a weekend night social gathering with alcohol rather than on a plaque for the retiring cafeteria supervisor. The dorm greets this idea with a crescendo of approval and finally someone stands up and screams, "Let's . . .

    a) fornicate!"
    b) party!"
    c) learn the Dewey
       Decimal System!"

Can you tell which one is not like the others?

Some expressions are rarely found around the universities.

4) Larry had been bragging to his frat brothers all week about how he was going to ask Janet to the frat formal. At week's end, Larry dressed up as a knight in shining armor and dropped to one knee to request the hand of the fair Janet. Said she in a haughty tone,"I don't care for medieval goons." Tony snickered, and said,"Larry, you got . . .

    a) change for a dollar?"
    b) Monday's problem
       set?"
    c) FACED !"

a) "like wow, man"
b) "blow it off"
c) "this is definitely hot!"
d) "she freaked out!"
e) "we're talking megabucks"
f) "eat your squash, Billy!"

Word Search

Find the words below using the clues.

1) Campus visitor who can't find stadium on map.
2) The last to know about the campus scandal.
3) Someone who thinks dorm food is good.
4) Dorm dork.
5) "Sans" clue.
6) Without clue.
7) Unable to solve this word search.

C	L	U	C	L	C
L	C	E	C	E	L
U	E	S	U	S	U
E	U	S	L	S	E
L	L	E	C	E	L
E	U	S	L	C	E
S	C	L	U	S	S
S	L	E	E	S	S

Prominent People

You see them on walls and doors. You watch them in movies and games, you listen to them on records, you read about them in books, magazines, and newspapers. They're the superstars, the heroes, the idols . . .the people whose posters you might put above your bed or whose example you might follow.

See if you can match the descriptions on the left with the prominent people on the right.

1) He smiles. He waves. He wears a cap and dresses in white. He never hurts anybody and his wish is that everybody love each other. Great hero for someone who wants to go into religion, or sell clothes at Macy's.

2) In the 60's, students admired her as a political activist. In the 70's, students admired her as an actress. Now, in the 80's, she's popular as an exercise guru. No truth to the rumor that she'll marry Richard Simmons.

3) Film director. Funny and Jewish.

4) Film director. Not Funny. Not Jewish.

5) Oppressed for years, he's so brilliant that he won a Nobel Prize, and somehow got away with naming a book The Gulag Archipelago. Name is very difficult to spell.

6) Great figure to shock your parents with. Does nine-hour concerts singing about his girlfriend whom he got pregnant in the back seat of a beat-up Chevy in a New Jersey parking lot.

7) He's good-looking. In fact, he's really good-looking. Okay, he's the greatest-looking guy ever in the history of mankind. Very popular with women.

8) Sort of a Third World Pope before his death in 1981. Sang about love and peace while spreading the Rastafarian message of world revolution through marijuana smoking. Not too popular in North Dakota.

9) Owner of Karen Miller's Beauty Salon.

    a. Bob Marley
    b. Alexander Solzhenitzyn
    c. Gloria Steinem
    d. Magic Johnson
    e. Francis Ford Coppola
    f. Jane Fonda
    g. Karen Miller
    h. Bruce Springsteen
    i. The Pope
    j. James Bond
    k. Pat Benatar
    l. Robert Redford
    m. Albert Einstein
    n. Woody Allen
    o. Buck Owens
    p. Christie Brinkley
    q. Elvis Costello
    r. Allah

Answers: 1i; 2f; 3n; 4e; 5b; 6h; 7d,j,l,m,o,q,r; 8a; 9g.

While You Were Out

Half of the adventure of living together with roommates is getting along with different people and sharing things with kids you've never met before. This is usually a great experience, but occasionally you'll encounter some minor hassles. One usual area of concern is the monthly phone bill.

Somehow, you'll end up with a call or two on your bill which no one will claim, and if it's a 15 dollar call to Montreal, you may have to play house detective. For practice, see if you can match the calls with the roommates on the following phone bill. Clues about each student are given below.

RON:
serious girlfriend back home
spends money freely

PETE:
serious girlfriend back home
thrifty
big sports fan

JIM:
drug dealer
rock music fan

CLARK:
no girlfriend back home
no close friends from high school
bad relationship with parents

 Pacific Telephone

PAGE ONE OF TWO

415-327-6872

DEC 11, 1982

DATE--TIME--MIN	*	PLACE AND NUMBER CALLED	CHARGE
10-22 9:00P 22	DE	BOGOTA, COLOMBIA 57-034913722	$ 36.20
10-23 11:01P 55	DN	CINCINNATI, OHIO 513-274-1501	$ 9.97
10-24 10:00A 197	DD	DALLAS, TEXAS 214-773-6952	$ 87.32
10-26 9:00P 22	DE	BOGOTA, COLOMBIA 57-034913722	$ 36.20
10-27 11:02P 57	DN	CINCINNATI, OHIO 513-274-1501	$ 10.33
10-30 10:00P 1	DE	SAN JOSE, CALIFORNIA 408-867-5309	$ .20
10-30 10:01P 1	DE	SEATTLE, WASHINGTON 206-867-5309	$ .39
10-30 10:02P 1	DE	ST.LOUIS, MISSOURI 314-867-5309	$ .41
10-30 10:03P 1	DE	ALBANY, OREGON 503-867-5309	$ .39
11-2 9:00P SERV	DE	SPORTS SERVICE 900-976-1313	$ .50
11-3 11:01P 54	DN	CINCINNATI, OHIO 513-274-1501	$ 9.79
11-5 8:47A 233	DD	DALLAS, TEXAS 214-773-6952	$103.16

| | | | | $267.46 |

Answers:

RON:
Dallas calls: *indiscriminately calls Caroline and talks forever.*

PETE:
Short, cheap, late-night calls to Cincinnati: *always calls Betty Lou after 11:00*
900-976-1313 (sports line): *gotta have that Reds score.*

JIM:
Bogota calls: *Colombian connections.*
All 867-5309 calls: *late night phone games inspired by drugs and Tommy Tutone.*

CLARK:
None. Occasionally orders a pizza, but that's a local call.

Notes To A Guy With A Car

It's great to have a car at college. You can get off campus to see shows, concerts, and sports events; you can eat at nice restaurants; you can escape whenever you feel like it. But be careful; if you're one of the few kids with wheels in the dorm, you'll probably be besieged night and day with requests for your car.

THREE

GET
SMART

EDUCATIONAL ASPECTS OF COLLEGE

Traditionally, college has been Socratic in its reputation for teaching and questioning. The four years at the university are meant to help the student to question life, question the environment, and question his or her direction. Through the process of taking classes, choosing a major, and pondering a career, the undergraduate leaves college with a firm grip on the present and a keen eye toward the future with much learning still ahead.

In classes, you'll begin to analyze, and then form opinions of, the grading procedures and your profs. Grades create pressure. To relieve some of the pressure, a number of institutions offer a pass/no credit option for the entire freshman year and some offer the opportunity of dropping classes very late in the semester. A few have even abolished the "F"; if a student fails a class, the grade simply never appears on the transcript. Though these devices have succeeded in relieving grade pressure at some places, they have also contributed to grade inflation. Some educators maintain that students are not being treated harshly enough and that there is no incentive for making good grades because everyone else is making them, too. The suicide rate has gone down, however.

No matter how idealistic you or your professors are about the college learning process, the importance of grades cannot be denied. Grad schools seem to look at your grades before they even look at your name, and schools with no grades foster competition among students with the "teacher reports" that are submitted instead.

You'll also wonder about your professors and try to figure out just what they do. The classic function of the college professor is two-fold: to teach and do research in his or her chosen field. If a professor ever wants to get tenure, he or she must do both well, but it often seems that teaching takes a back seat. After all, the old adage is "publish or perish," not "teach or impeach." That's why professors often seem brilliant, driven, and somewhat aloof. After all, how would you like to spend your life studying the Abelard effect on medieval asceticism?

Or even worse, how would you like to teach your life's work to several dozen beer-guzzling preppies who think medieval means "not too bad?" No wonder professors are so eccentric. There are exceptions, of course. There's that occasional professor who really seems to love students and enjoy teaching. That prof probably won't get tenure.

Within your first two years at college, you'll pick a major. The major you choose will reflect your academic interests, strengths, and possibly future career orientation. Not only is it all right to change majors in the last two years, it is quite common. If you are thinking about changing majors and you're a senior or a junior, just remember the few each year who change majors in the last few weeks and still graduate.

Making The Grade

You should realize by now that college and high school differ in dozens of way, but no one difference is more pronounced than grading. Before you begin to take classes, you need to know the intricacies of grading in college.

1) **The Curve.** In college, grading is based on a "curve" system which means most of the class will receive a "B" or "C". Therefore, you'll probably receive a "B" or a "C".

2) **Exams.** Most college courses have final exams which count as a considerable portion of your grade. This means that you can blow most of your work until the last week or so and still do okay. Students have been known to miss every class, skip all the reading, take only the final exam, and get a "B". Still, other students have been known to miss every class, skip all the reading, not take the final exam, and get an "F".

3) **Incompletes.** Many schools have a policy of postponing a student's grade in a class to the next quarter or even the next year. These postponements, known as incompletes, usually require a medical excuse, but you'll be surprised how easy it is to come down with rabies the night before a 25 page term paper is due.

Anatomy of An A

If getting an A in high school seemed difficult, getting one in college may often border on the impossible. Still, there are students who seem to get A's consistently. Some of these students are hard workers and actually study two hours for each hour in class. But most don't. They use modern methods for getting A's. Try one of these GPA raising tactics.

1) **Study with good students.** Invite them over and serve them some wine. Pretty soon, they'll be telling you everything.

2) **Talk to the prof after class.** Since most of your fellow students are in slumberland by the time a lecture ends, you can get a jump on them by bounding up to the professor and telling him how much you enjoyed his lecture on Glacial Effluvial Outwash.

3) **Take the professor to lunch.** Spend a lot and he'll think you're worth getting to know. Casually mention that you loved his last book.

4) **Attend a professor's office hours.** No one else ever does, so the professor will think you actually care about the subject.

5) **Name your newborn child after your professor.** This takes a spouse, some planning, and enough nerve to name your kid "Phinias" or "Gwendelyn."

A Touch of Classes

The first step on the long road to graduation begins when you obtain a copy of the college Courses and Degrees book. This publication will summarize each class offered and aid you in your academic planning for the semester. However, it also makes every class sound interesting and educational, when in fact many are boring and bland.

While skimming through your Courses and Degrees manual, try to "see through" some of the class summaries.

HISTORY

100A - History of the World
Prof. Young
Globe Auditorium

A history of the world from its inception to the present.

100F - King Rudolph the Red
Prof. Donner
Blitzen Room

An in-depth look at the obscure "Reindeer King" of Botslavia, and speculation as to the significance of his famous Christmas disappearances.

LANGUAGE

101 - Beginning Californian
Prof. Brown
Somebody's Jacuzzi

A not-too-fast, rather mellow introduction to the Californian languages. Course structure includes work on vocabulary and inflections, as well as exploration of alternative lifestyles. No class limit. No prerequisites. No books. Whatever.

COMMUNICATION

115 - Let's Communicate!
Suzi
On the lawn

How and why we communicate! Special attention to body talk, signals, and positive/negative vibes! Lots of workshops! Rap sessions! Only one requirement: a sense of adventure!

ENGINEERING

100 - Introduction to Success
Prof. Resume
Security Hall

Teaches students how to manage a $32,000 starting salary. Subjects covered include check writing, stocks and bonds, real estate, tax loopholes, retirement. For engineering majors only.

BIOLOGY

002 - Creating New Life
Prof. Nobel *DNA Building*

Students are required to genetically engineer a new human being. No prerequisites.

ENGLISH

200F - Fifth Century Novels
Prof. Recondite
Arcane Hall

Course delves deeply into both novels written in the fifth century.

ECONOMICS

112D - The Economics of Poverty
Prof. Reagan
White House

Small group colloquium for wealthy students. Study of a hypothetical nation which implements a new economic policy detrimental to anyone with an annual income of less than $40,000 a year.

COMPUTER SCIENCE

113B - English as a Second Language
Prof. Realworld
Life Building

Class introduces Computer Science majors to more advanced skills with the English Language. Students will progress to the point where they will actually be able to converse normally with people outside of the Computer Science field.

Selected Seminars

Self Improvement

Guilt without Sex
Ego Gratification through Violence
Whine your way to Alienation
How to Overcome Self-Doubt through Pretense and Ostentation

Business and Career

The Underachievers Guide to Very Small Business Opportunties
Money Can Make You Rich
"How I Made $100 in Real Estate"
Packaging and Selling Your Roommate
Looters' Guide to America's Cities

Home Economics

How You Can Convert Your Family Room into a Garage
Burglarproof Your Home with Concrete
How to Convert a Wheelchair into a Dune Buggy
1001 Other Uses for Your Vacuum Cleaner

Crafts

Needlecraft for Junkies
Gifts for the Senile

Health and Fitness

Creative Tooth Decay
Tap Dance Your Way to Social Ridicule
Understanding Nudity
Skate Yourself to Regularity

Blowing It Off

Got a paper due? Need to read 700 pages of medieval history over the weekend? Too much work and not enough time? You need the one word solution: procrastination.

Procrastination may at first seem wasteful, purposeless, and a bit immoral. After all, haven't you always been taught "don't put off till tomorrow what you can do today?" Haven't you seen what happens to the cricket who doesn't save for the winter and needs to beg from the ant?

What about the tortoise and the hare? The choice seems simple. It's not quite so simple in reality, however, when you have to choose between a tall cool one and 257 pages of Leibnitz. Hell, Leibnitz probably would have chosen the tall cool one.

Still, it's hard to escape your past. That's why when you procrastinate in college, you have to have a worthwhile objective in mind. Consider these mature alternatives:

Writing letters. Thank God for procrastination; otherwise, you'd never write your parents. A recent study has shown that letter writing is directly proportional to amount of work due.

Deciding whether to go to the library. This can take hours. If you go to the library you might see all of your friends so you wouldn't get any work done. On the other hand, if you stay in the dorm, you know that you won't get any work done. But the lights in the library give you a headache. But the noise in the dorm gives you a headache. But it's hot in the library. But there are too many distractions in the dorm. But the library is clear across campus. But . . .

Going to the Library. Look for someone in the dorm to go with you. Walk instead of rid-

Real Testimony from
A Guy Who Procrastinates

Lemme tell ya' somethin' . . . deadlines don't matter. They don't matter at all. I blew off plenty of 'em, and I still got damned good grades.

They're for woosies, lemmings - you know, the kind of people who acutally follow directions. The GREAT people make their own deadlines.

An' lemme tell ya' one more thing: some profs will give you a better grade if you blow 'em off. Proves you have a mind of your own. I just turned in a paper for Freshmen English. The instructor's dead now, but I bet I get an A.

15 Ways to Say You're Sleeping

The true procrastinator has an imagination. He doesn't just sleep, he does it in style. To help you impress your friends while losing touch with reality, here is a start on building your college vocab.

1) Bagging Z's
2) Catching Forty Winks
3) Catching Some Shut-Eye
4) Crashing
5) Hugging the Crib
6) Interviewing the Sandman
7) Sacking Out
13) Sleeping
14) Snoozing
15) Z-ing

ing your bike. Take time searching for a perfect place to study (that should swallow a good half hour). When finally settled, go get a drink of water. Then reach for a magazine.

Reading magazines. You've got to know what's going on in the world, don't you? Who was in charge of the recent Serbo-Croatian economic sanctions on Albania? What's Timothy Hutton's latest film about? These are very important questions that demand an immediate answer. The ten page paper can wait.

Running errands. "Let's see .- . . new bike tire, dry cleaners, coffee, wash the car . . . shouldn't take more than an hour. Then I can start my paper." Guaranteed to kill at least three hours. Don't go out with an unbalanced checkbook, though.

Balancing checkbook. How are you supposed to do your paper if you might be overdrawn at the bank? Isn't your credit rating more important than a five page essay? Besides, it gives you a chance to finally use the calculator that you got for Christmas.

Rearranging/cleaning/fixing room. If you're like most people, you need a nice room if you are to study. Clean it up a little. Clean the desk out while you're at it. Why stop there? Rearrange the furniture; that will give you a better study attitude. And while you're at it, you might as well put up those stereo shelves you've been thinking about. Maybe it's time to knock out that wall and annex the room next door.

Philosophical discussion. Certainly the single most potent force in the history of college procrastination. Enables you to find out more about yourself, to become closer to potential lifelong friends, and to pass the hour while you wait for the pizza.

Calling old friends. This is an especially great procrastination device because it enables two people in different locations to blow off their work simultaneously. Both of you can whine about how you have too much work and too little time.

Hitting The Books

A large part of college is spent studying. It's important to pick a place that's right for you when you're ready to get down to the books. Too distracting and you may not get anything done. Too quiet and you may go crazy. Too comfortable and you may fall asleep. No matter how attractive a place may seem at first, there always seem to be enough drawbacks to keep you from getting any work done.

The Library. If your school has one main undergraduate library, then chances are it will be like Grand Central Station during prime studying hours. Friends meeting friends, enemies avoiding enemies - everything but studying goes on here. A good place to go when you want to feel less guilty about not studying, but not so great for getting things done.

Your Room. It's late afternoon, still an hour or so till dinner. The dorm is quiet, and you think that now would be a perfect time to get a little studying in. Wrong. Either your roommate will come in from lacrosse practice, throw her stuff on the ground, and crank Springsteen, or you'll be lulled into bed "just to lie down for a minute or two" and sleep through dinner.

Outside While Tanning. How many times do you have to try this to realize that it's just not possible? You keep looking down at your arms and stomach to make sure they're not burning, and people are running and talking all around you. The glare from your book is so intense you can't read a word. Hardly a studious environment.

In an Empty Room on Campus. Not a bad choice. It's a studious and quiet atmosphere and because you're alone there will be few distractions. On the other hand, you'll probably start hearing a tone in your head when you read, little buzzing noises from the lights, and potential mass murderers walking by outside. You'll probably end up going back to the library where you'll at least be safe.

Coffee, Tea, or . . .

Once you get to college, the days of sacking out at ll o'clock are over, but your body doesn't know that. That's where stimulants come in handy. With the right pill or drink, you can stay up all night, finishing an important paper, book, or conversation.

Coffee. Easily the most popular stimulant. Used in offices as the official wake-up drug, this drink has a social acceptance that makes it apropos virtually all the time. Some people drink so much of it that they seem to have a coffee cup grafted to their hand.

Tea. For those who won't admit that they're caffeine addicts. You can still maintain a certain elegance while sucking down as much caffeine as the chain smoking slob next to you. People who have studied in Britain always come back drinking tea.

Coke (Coca-Cola) or most other carbonated beverages. Second only to coffee in acceptance, you have to drink twice as much to get the same kick. Causes gastro-intestinal problems, but if you're tired and thirsty, try this.

Coke (Cocaine). REALLY keeps you awake. Unless you're in Beverly Hills, this isn't quite as socially acceptable as coffee, but it's a lot more fun. The problem is calming down enough to work on the paper. You may have to take out a loan to afford it.

No-Doz. Concentrated caffeine in a pill, this stuff will keep you going into next semester. You'll probably have to start taking sleeping pills to ever get to sleep again.

The All Nighter

Savior to many and unexperienced by few, this panacea has come to the aid of millions of students in their hours of need over four years (remember that night when a 10 a.m. deadline was reminding you of a five page paper on a 400 page book which you hadn't even opened?). After staring at the clock for hours, drowning in pots of coffee, procrastinating with everyone in the hall, and waking up two days later feeling as though they had slept in a washing machine, most students decide to leave the All Nighter as a last resort. Curiously enough, some cherish it as a first resort.

There are numerous aids to help you on your All Nighter, but if it's your first time, be gentle. Some critics claim the All Nighter was a creation of the No-Doz public relations department, but the truth is that it has been around since the dawn of time. Did you know that the following were actually blown off till the last minute and completed in one night?

FAMOUS ALL NIGHTERS
1) Stonehenge
2) Michelangelo's *David*
3) Leo Tolstoy's
   War and Peace
4) Brooklyn Bridge
5) City of Rome
   (They're right; it wasn't
   built in a day).

Testing Your Nerves

What would college be without exams? Most likely, pure unadulterated fun. But since you have to take exams, you might as well plod through each class taking copious notes, head to the library cursing all the way, and carefully study each pen stroke of those notes. In the exam room, perspire heavily thinking about what Dad's going to say if this grade crushes all hopes for law school. Panic wildly when you see the questions. Scribble intensely about anything related. Don't cheat unless you must. To hang on at the end, ramble, and if you don't think you're going to have time to finish, prepare an appeal mentally, assuring yourself that everyone will be doing the same. Exit relieved and confident that you did at least as well as everyone else.

College exams don't have to be this way. In fact, four out of five professors surveyed recommend acing for their student who must get into law school. Acing is a simple three step procedure: 1) Enter the exam room and sit down in a comfortable chair; 2) Pick up exam booklets and fill out name, date, and course number; 3) Answer all questions correctly. Incidentally, the fifth professor surveyed recommends not taking his class.

Sample: **English**

What you'll see in the exam room

Q. In one of his lesser known works, *Frosty: As It Were*, William Shakespeare protrays the emergence of the snowman in contemporary society and its relevance to the existence of children. In 329 words or fewer, relate the significance of the top hat to current world events and describe how you would have reacted if a loved one had joined the famous snowman cult. Would you have gone to Frostyville? Explain.

And what you'll write

A. In Shakespeare's time, the snowman represented _____ and
                                                       (noun)
consequently_____ the inability to bifurcate. In
             (verb)
_____, it was not natural to _____ in public. However,
(year)   (verb)
Frosty_____the children with his _____ ,
  (verb past)   (noun)

while they _____ sought to escape the _____
   (adverb)   (person adjective)
world in which they were trapped. _____ , so
           (phrase)
Frosty provided _____ , though in an existential world he
      (noun)
would have supplied _____ . This
        (noun or leave blank)
was referred to as _____ .
   (person 'ism')

using such variables as

Ergo   Hence   Heretofore
Albeit   Thus   Stereotype

Planning the Day

High School

7:00-7:30am:	Wake up
7:30-8:00am:	Breakfast
8:00-3:00pm:	School
3:00-5:00pm:	Practice
5:00-6:00pm:	Watch news
6:00-7:00pm:	Dinner
7:00-8:00pm:	Watch TV
8:00-9:30pm:	Phone friends
9:30-10:00pm:	Homework
10:00pm:	Bed

College (ideally)

7:00-7:30am:	Wake up
7:30-8:00am:	Breakfast
8:00-12:00am:	Classes
12:00-1:00pm:	Lunch
1:00-4:00pm:	Study
4:00-5:00pm:	Athletics
5:00-6:00pm:	Dinner
6:00-12:00am:	Study
12:00am:	Bed

College (really)

10:30-11:30am:	Wake up
11:45-12:00pm:	Class
12:00-1:00pm:	Lunch
1:00-2:00pm:	Play music, make bed
2:00-3:00pm:	Watch soap opera
3:00-4:00pm:	Sports
4:00-5:00pm:	Wait around for dinner
5:00-6:00pm:	Dinner
6:00-9:00pm:	Sit and talk after dinner
9:00-11:00pm:	See movie on campus
11:00-11:30pm:	Order pizza
11:30-12:00am:	Get book to study
12:00-3:00am:	Talk with friends
3:00 am:	Sack

As it were	John Keats	Neo-ism
As it is	Platonic	Anything related to
As it has been	Neoplatism	a philosopher or 'neo'
Up to this point in time		
Displays the manifestation of itself as		
Or a reasonable facsimile thereof		
The Great Elizabethean Towel Shift		

Sample: **Political Science**

Don't freak out when you see

Q. The British Empire was as much a result of Anglo-Saxon thirst for global power, of Britain's lack of natural resources, and of jealousy of her neighbors' colonial acquistions as it was of Queen Victoria's insatiable hunger for grilled cheese sandwiches. Explain.

Just write

A. The British have always been _____ , so it would make
                                   (adj.)

sense   that _____ could force them into _____ instead
              (noun pl.)   (gerund)
of hiring new groundkeepers. The _____ effect of the outdoor
                                   (adj.)
grill on world cheese supplies led the _____ to
                                        (nationality)
_____ preemptively before it was too _____ . It was true
 (verb)   (adj.)
that the _____ were challenging the British at
          (nationality above)
_____ , but Queen Victoria abhorred _____
(outdoor activity)   (noun)
due to her dislike of badminton, vis-a-vis _____ .
                                            (food)

using

Vis-a-vis	Hegemony	Juxtaposed
Hoi polloi	Proletariat	Once
Plethora	A Priori	Twice
Haig	Bosom Buddies	Three times a lady
Halitosis	Memory Lane	The SAT
Asymmetrical interdependence		Cluster block analyses

Danger: Influential Books Ahead

Although nearly all learning achieved at college turns out to be beneficial, there are some aspects of education which have questionable results. For example, influential books have been plaguing students for years. If your high school background in great works of literature is minimal, be careful that an influential book you read at college doesn't change your life too drastically.

If you're still a bit confused, take a look at the following examples.

Case 1

Name: Joe Normal
Home: Carbondale, Illinois

Background/Achievements: Senior Class Council, School Newspaper, Industrial Arts Student Award, Cross Country, Track, Young Life, Fellowship of Christian Athletes.
High School Reading: Red Badge of Courage, Popular Mechanics, Contemporary Christianity, half of Call of the Wild, The Bible, How to Build Your Own Datsun.

Influential Book Read in College: The Stranger by Albert Camus.

Case History: 10/1 College be-gins; 10/20 Other students report strange attitude changes; 10/25 Begins speaking French; 10/29 Shoots foreign graduate student on beach trip; 11/3 Arrested and jailed; 11/8 Renounces God; 11/10 Hanged; enjoys death.

Case 2

Name: Bitsy Buckingham
Home: Bellevue, Washington
Background/Achievements: Homecoming Queen, ASB Treasurer, Head Cheerleader, Ski Club Treasurer, Miss Teenage Washington.
High School Reading: Glamour, anything by Harold Robbins, How to Invest Money, Dior's Guide to Jewelry, The Krugerrand and You.

Influential Book Read in College: Utopia by Thomas More.

Case History: 9/10 College begins; 10/5 Burns Republican Party card; 10/10 Calls father and urges divestiture of South African holdings; 10/17 Begins giving clothes and jewelry to poor roommate; 10/24 Writes $100 checks to every minority on campus; 10/30 Gives away all worldly possessions; 11/3 Joins obscure cult and sails to South America. (Never heard from again.)

The Problem With Tests

Many college exams must be written in essay form. When you sit down to take the exam, the first thing you'll realize is that you don't know where to begin. This problem may happen to you often if you never study for exams and don't have the faintest idea of how to begin. The secret in knowing where to start lies in the exam question itself.

History. Write a lot, but make sure what you write is completely true. Repeat the question a few times in your essay.

Q. In Churchill's *The Gathering Storm*[a] we learn that the second world war[b] was unavoidable.[c] How does this coincide with our perception of the imminence of WWIII?

[a] Even if you haven't read the book, you shouldn't panic. From the title you can infer that *Storm* probably means **war**, and *Gathering* implies **imminent.**

[b] Repeat this a few times, as well as: WWII, World War Two, the Big One, Double U Double U Two, and Hitler's Baby.

[c] Use this word often, also, along with: unavoided, unavoidance, not able to be avoided, and clearly not avoidable.

- Haven't been to class recently? Don't worry; since WWIII hasn't occurred yet, you can conceivably write anything, but avoid the following subjects:
    The declining role of the professor in society.
    The phasing out of government funding for history departments.
    History: the doomed major.
    The history professor's imminent trip to the end of the unemployment line.

Religion. The analysis of this sample question below tells all.

Q. Using your knowledge of Hinduism, Islam, Judaism, and Christianity, discuss whether or not God exists.

Start with the "God" spelled backwards is "Dog" analysis. Point out that in German "God" is "Gott" which when spelled backwards (Ttog) has no meaning, hence the existential significance of the German language. End by theorizing that if God doesn't exist, why do so many women cry out for him in the throes of orgasmic climax?

Physics. Strictly for people who know what they're doing.

Q. If the total force applied to the rock pictured below equals its shadow weight, or

$$\int_0^b \frac{ZY}{x^3}\, d(x) = F(my^2)$$

how much nuclear energy would be needed to produce 23 KWhr if there are 213 db and it is 59 (degrees) C?

Equally important in test taking is knowing when to drop the class.

Cliff's Movies

When you've blown off the whole week knowing full well that the ten pager was due Monday, and you've even dared to go to the Sunday Night Flicks, there's nothing quite as comforting as Cliff's Notes. Although literary briefs like Cliff's Notes are universally frowned upon by English profs, they're easy to rationalize. After all, why reinvent the wheel? Somebody more intelligent has already read the book and painstakingly detailed its worth.

Overwhelming demand for Cliff's, Monarch, and other merciful timesavers (not to mention lifesavers) has enticed companies to diversify. Soon to appear in college bookstores are Cliff's Labs (for the pre-med on the go), Monarch Paintings (for the busy Art Historian without the time to go gallery hopping), Monarch Encyclopedias, and, lastly, Cliff's Movies. Although still in the testing stages, Cliff's Movies will be available soon on videodisk and will save the average student countless hours. Imagine War and Peace reduced from ten hours to ten minutes, Gone with the Wind to three minutes, and Fellini's La Strada cut to 29 seconds! Their success lies in the removal of all unnecessary scenes, such as pointless walking, worthless banter, and ordinary battle scenes. What's left is a compendium of rousing cries, plunging knives, climactic kisses and, of course, The End.

Test Givers

When it comes to *giving* exams, many professors can be categorized. See if you can find your own profs among these stereotypes.

1) Mr. Casual. This guy gives exams because they're part of the curriculum. Everyone in the class can predict the exam questions; sometimes he reveals them in advance. He's satisfied with his sex life and his two cars in the garage. Score points by asking him about his weekend up north.

2) The Challenger. She believes that exams should stimulate the mind and be learning experiences in themselves. She couldn't pass her own exams if she tried, but don't mention this to her. If you've studied, never fear. If you haven't, turn to "Transferring" or "What to do about a ruined transcript."

3) Mr. Nasty. He hasn't been the same since third grade when Bobby Johnson beat him to a pulp at recess. He feels it's his duty to single-handedly lower grade inflation. As popular as the bubonic plague. Curves on a C.

4) The Grade Inflator. Tries to be the most popular prof on campus. Succeeds. Take all his classes. Curves his tests on an A-. Greatest guy in the world.

Test Takers

Likewise, many students can be categorized when it comes to *taking* exams. See if you can find your dormmates among these stereotypes.

The Challenger. She has a point to make. Scores points by implying exams are learning experiences in themselves. Tries to turn question on professor, however, and loses points. Not popular due to pseudo-intellectual air and ABBA album collection.

Ms. Casual. She takes exams because they're part of the curriculum. Popular because she's not a red hot. She'll probably go into teaching grammar school. Before going to an exam she'll read the newspaper or call a friend from high school.

The Grade Inflator. Only person smiling during reading period. Everyone loves him. Throws parties. Goes drinking night before exam. Lowers curve. Great guy.

Red Hot. High GPA. In fact, very high GPA. Reads the recommended books. Pitches tent beside study carrel. Reviews notes with one hand while at urinal. For study break, he goes to dinner.

Questions and Comments

The more creative students sometimes think that instructors must get bored grading all of those papers that deal with dry topics such as "Canto V of Dante's Inferno as an Image of Dante's Christian-Humanist Tendencies." Surely the professor would enjoy something different, something funny. Just because he has a PhD in 13th century Italian Literature doesn't mean that he wasn't the class clown in 7th grade. Why, he probably throws parties where he serves his colleagues wine out of dribble glasses, and deftly places whoopie cushions on the chairs. He's probably dying for a good laugh.

The truth is that the college professor has not spent ten years studying an obscure subject just to become a professor, make less money than a bulldozer operator, and read a paper making fun of his life's work. His object is to let you know that he is MUCH smarter than you, and he didn't get there by telling jokes.

In Title Only

Books may not be judged by their cover, but you'd better believe that college papers are judged by their titles. When you're a poor graduate student getting paid $3.50 an hour to grade the papers for Freshman Composition, you'll understand. Paper after paper with titles like "Symbolism in Huck Finn" or "To Be or Not To Be" can make you weary, if not physically ill. An imaginative title can turn a boring essay into an enticing invitation and can also train you to write for papers like "The National Enquirer." The following suggested titles should get you started.

DEATH
MURDER CAN BE FUN
CATHERINE THE
GREAT'S WILD RIDE
SHAKESPEARE:Gay?
YES, WE HAVE NO
BANANAS:
An Analysis of Freud
THE BIBLE WAS WRONG

To Hell With Dante

by Claude Jones

You're in a beautiful green meadow with this

nice-looking lady. The birds are chirping, a sub-

We have no evidence of this.

tle zephyr wafts through the trees, making her

nipples slightly erect and quite palpable, espe-

cially through the skimpy blouse she has on. What

13th century garb hardly provided for this.

do you expect the guy to do? So anyway, Paolo (the

guy) has just happened to bring along this book

about Sir Lancelot. Was this guy smooth or what?

Francesca (the chick) falls for it; they read the

Francesca was fowl?

book and they get to the part where Lancelot and

Guinevere get down and before you know it Paolo

Ambiguous

and Francesca go at it. Who can blame 'em? So

Clear Boethian question of guilt in the universe.

they're having a great time when who shows up but

Francesca's hubby. He decides he's going to be a

party-pooper (he probably had a bad day at the

office) so he hatchets them to death. Dante meets

them in Hell. Can you believe that? They put a

guy that smooth in Hell. Guess we don't have to

worry though, eh Professor Marshall? Anyway,

Speak for yourself!

Dante swoons and Francesca talks and Paolo cries

and Virgil just stands there as usual (kind of

like Wally on "Leave It To Beaver") and the whole

Actually, Wally represents a Nietzschean superman: read Turner's book Wally Cleaver, Nietzsche and Hemingway.

thing is a big waste of time.

(B+) Claude—

you develop the characters well, but you do not go far enough in your assertion that Paolo was smooth. Why not mention his jacuzzi? Or his Mercedes? As far as you go, however, this paper is concise, direct and interesting.

On Thy Honor

Hundreds of schools have honor codes and perhaps your school, too, has a parchment of truth and justice, exhorting you to lead an honest life at least while in the academic world. Some codes are written in seemingly endless flourishes of legal eminence, while others put it simply. In both cases the message is: *don't cheat.*

Almost all honor codes include a phrase or two obliging you to "report any infringements of the word of the code hereof"; translation: if you see someone cheating, tell us. Nobody ever does. You won't either. Who could be bothered?

CREATIVE TEST TAKING

Seventy-five percent of all students polled have admitted to cheating at least once during their college career, yet very few are caught. How are students getting away with it? The answer becomes clear when you examine the various methods used.

One ironic facet of cheating is that it requires as much time to prepare an aid as it does to study. Cheating, however, provides the desperate student with a tangible crutch to help in the hour of need.

Old Standbys

1) Notes in the shoes, on the cuffs, on pens, in palm. Not very original, and, frankly, very boring.

2) Obtain copy of test in advance; use as a study aid. This old favorite of frats comes in handy if you can't decide which material to study.

3) "Lose test." While in exam room, eat exam or stuff it in pockets. When the prof or T.A. tells you your exam got lost, look distraught and tell him how hard you studied for the test. Should be good for a C.

4) Crib sheets in bathroom. Excuse yourself "to go to the bathroom." That's exactly what you'll be doing, but not to use the plumbing.

New Imagination

1) Notes on sticks of chewing gum. You'll find you're able to fit the entire Gettysburg Address on only one stick of Juicy Fruit. If a proctor comes by, start chewing.

2) Obtain copy of test in advance; complete and bring to exam. Pretend to write for the first ten minutes. Then turn in and leave early, mumbling about how easy the test was.

3) "Lose test." Stuff exam in pockets and bring home to complete. Have a friend mail the completed exam to the prof with an accompanying note explaining how he or she had discovered the exam on the sidewalk outside the prof's house.

4) Desk in bathroom. Excuse yourself to go to the bathroom. Then get in a little more studying. . . in comfort.

Advanced Creativity

A) Clicking pens in Morse Code. This one is difficult because it assumes so much: that both you and a friend know Morse Code, that the test is multiple choice, and that the clicking noise won't drive every other student up the wall. If you can pull it off you may be able to challenge the Honor Code with Morse Code.

B) Goodyear Blimp lighted display. The fee could be pretty high, but no one would ever suspect no matter how many times the blimp circled above.

C) Mini cassette player disguised as hearing aid. Fellow classmates, with looks of surprise, may ask you when you went deaf. The T.A. might inquire as to the strange device sticking in your ear. To both reply, "What?"

D) Spy Chalk. Sneak into classroom the day before to write notes on the blackboard with special infra-red chalk. Read notes during exam with special heat-sensitive glasses disguised as Vuarnets.

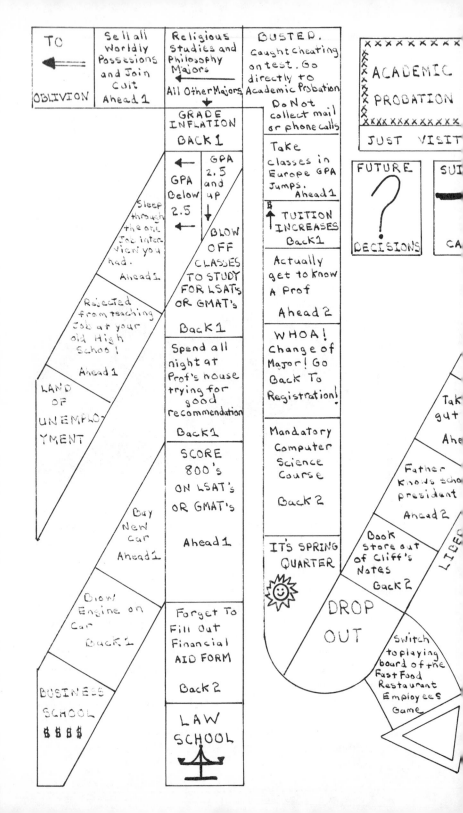

The Majors Game

As a part of "career planning," many high schools have implemented aptitude and psychology tests to help orient students toward a specific career goal. One of these modern tests is the "Playing Board Test." Since life often resembles a game, students are encouraged to simulate their future by playing the *College Majors Game*.

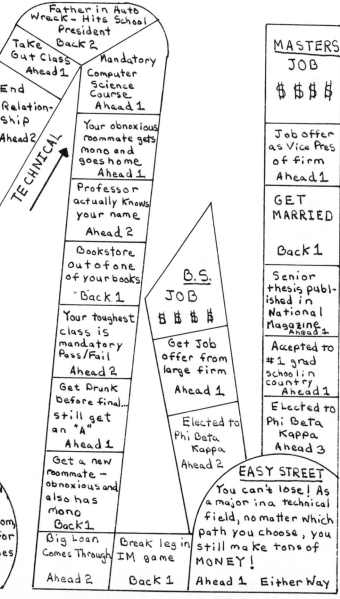

Pick the Prof

A job has just opened up in your college's Economics department. Hundreds have applied, but the faculty committee has narrowed that list to just two. Which of the two would you pick?

Dave Albertson
AGE: 32

EDUCATION:
U. of Minnesota undergraduate
U. of Oregon masters
U. of South Carolina PhD

EXPERIENCE:
TA at South Carolina
Assistant Professor, University of Kansas

PUBLISHED WORKS:
Three Novels
Econ Can Be Fun!
Where Is This Crazy Economy Going, Anyhow?
Slippery Curves: Advanced Econ

PERSONAL STATEMENT:
"Econ is a way of getting to know yourself through the people around you. It's sort of a cross between math and philosophy. To understand Keynes is to understand the world as we know it. I hope that my students come to love and respect the economics of everyday living, much more important than the economics found in textbooks."

C. Arthur Davidson
AGE: 57

EDUCATION:
Harvard undergraduate
Harvard Masters
Harvard PhD

EXPERIENCE:
TA Harvard
Full Professor, Bennington College, Bennington, VT.

PUBLISHED WORKS:
Five books
Ricardo and the Philosophers
Ricardo: Was He Right?
The Ricardian Treatise
A Look at Ricardo, the Man
Economics Under Ricardo

PERSONAL STATEMENT:
"Economics as we know it today is still an example of Ricardian theory in action."

Davidson got the job. Econ Director Stockman convinced the trustees that Davidson's knowledge of Ricardo could shed some light on the problem with today's troubled economy. Davidson was well liked, though at first the president of the university balked at courses devoted solely to the works of a Cuban band leader.

Albertson was turned down for tenure at Kansas and now lives off the royalties from his fourth book, a bestseller.

FOUR

WITHOUT
CLASS

EXTRA-CURRICULAR ACTIVITIES

Whether you're a great football player, an avid writer, or a future Sri Lankan weatherman, there is probably an extracurricular group for you. Most groups are easy to join, and give you a chance to take up a new hobby and meet new people. An extracurricular activity can be an escape from the rigors of study, or a chance to put classroom-acquired knowledge to practical use.

Academically-oriented extracurriculars are of a little higher quality in college than they were in high school. High School "English Club" is replaced by student magazines or newspapers in college. High school plays give way to fully orchestrated and choreographed college extravaganzas. High school debate topics like "The Dangers of Smoking" are usurped by such subjects as "The Everyday Rape of the American Woman."

Of course, most extracurricular activities are not academic in nature. There are dozens of athletic opportunities at most colleges, ranging from jogs with friends to nationally ranked intercollegiate sports. There is nothing quite like the excitement of a football game, even when you're too drunk to know what's going on.

In many ways, socially-oriented extracurricular organizations (especially fraternities and sororities) can be the most important of all because they provide you with social activities, housing, and a certain way of life. Once you've become a KA or a Kappa, people will expect you to act like a KA or a Kappa (whatever that means). Fraternities and sororities are often getting together for parties or mixers. Greek life can do wonders for your social calendar.

The university will tell you to remember that extracurriculars are only there to round out your schedule and help you study better. Whether this is true or not is debatable, but for one reason or another, almost everyone takes part in some kind of extracurricular activity while in college.

Getting Involved

The college community boasts an incredible number of student services and opportunities for involvement. Find the group that's right for you and join soon.

Outing club. We're a club organized for outings such as camping and canoeing. If you'd like to go on one of these trips and have a tent or a canoe or other stuff like that then let us know.

Young Democrats. We're organized to help serve our country through political awareness. Minorities welcome.

Young Republicans. We're organized to help serve our country through political awareness.

Student Government Association. Hey all you sloths!!! Don't be apathetic!! Did you know that the SGA is made up of each of you? Help support a better school! Join YOUR Student Government Association!!!

ROTC. Why pay all that money to go to school? In exchange for some calisthenics, a few classes, and four years of your life after graduation, the US government will pay tuition for you.

Young Philosophers. We're a club which may or may not exist and that may or may not matter. If you'd like, you can contact us.

Hari Krishna. We are a group of demented young loons who feature the latest in Eastern garb and sport Mohawk hairstyles. If you think you might be interested in tossing away all your worldly possessions, denying your heritage, and destroying any possible future you might have had, come join us at the corner of Fifth and Main.

Drama Club. "Life is a Cabaret, old chum, come to the Cabaret." That's a line from one of the many plays we put on last year. This year we're going to do "King Lear," "Sweeney Todd," "One Flew Over the Cuckoo's Nest," and "The Ten Commandments." BUT WE NEED HELP!!! Whether you're an experienced actor or a novice thespian, there's a place for you in the Drama Club.

The Campus Politico

After you've been part of a campus organization for a while, you may want to extend your involvement a little further. At most universities, the best way to do this is to run for a posi-

VOTE FOR SCOTT BECAUSE HE CAN RELATE!!

Hi, Suzy; 8 o'clock tonight?
Scott talks to his girlfriend

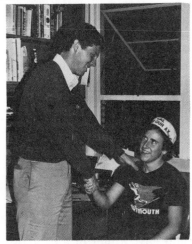

Yeah, I got some last night, and boy was I drunk!
Scott talks to his roommate

All right, Rafael brother, how many'd you get in last night's game?
Scott talks to a black man

tion in some branch of student government. A student who becomes involved in this is known as a "politico", and he or she usually becomes fairly well known around campus. The most important quality of a successful campus politico is the ability to understand the delicate make up of a diverse campus population.

That's a great looking calculator, Robert. Wow, sine functions!
Scott talks to a nerd

Hi, Omar, how's Exxon's stock?
Scott talks to an Arab

How's the old bitch?
Scott talks to a dog

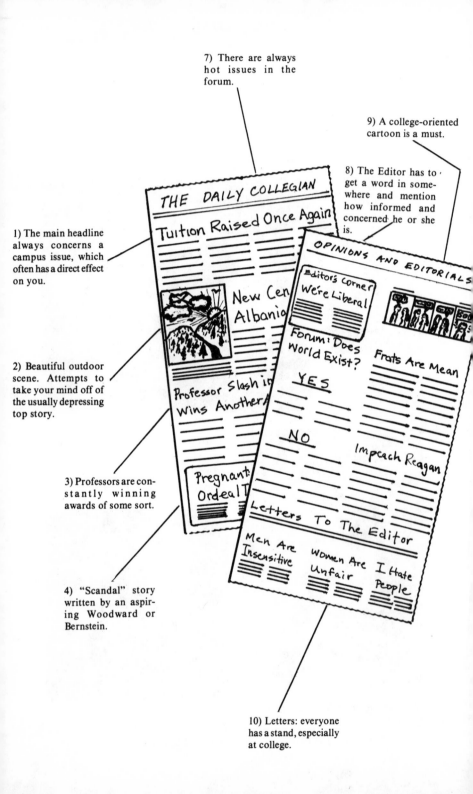

7) There are always hot issues in the forum.

9) A college-oriented cartoon is a must.

8) The Editor has to get a word in somewhere and mention how informed and concerned he or she is.

1) The main headline always concerns a campus issue, which often has a direct effect on you.

2) Beautiful outdoor scene. Attempts to take your mind off of the usually depressing top story.

3) Professors are constantly winning awards of some sort.

4) "Scandal" story written by an aspiring Woodward or Bernstein.

10) Letters: everyone has a stand, especially at college.

THE DAILY COLLEGIAN

Tuition Raised Once Again

New Cen
Albania

Professor Slash i
Wins Another

Pregnant
Ordeal T

OPINIONS AND EDITORIALS

Editor's Corner
We're Liberal

Forum: Does World Exist?

YES

NO

Frats Are Mean

Impeach Reagan

Letters To The Editor

Men Are Insensitive

Women Are Unfair

I Hate People

The School Paper

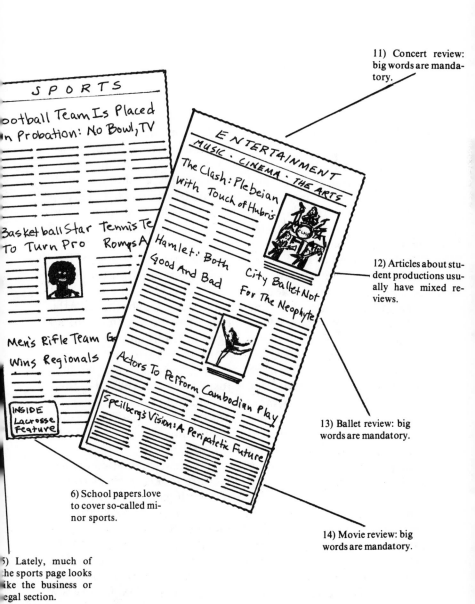

SPORTS

ootball Team Is Placed
n Probation: No Bowl, TV

Basketball Star   Tennis Te
To Turn Pro   Romps A

Men's Rifle Team G
Wins Regionals

INSIDE
Lacrosse
Feature

ENTERTAINMENT
MUSIC · CINEMA · THE ARTS

The Clash: Plebeian
With Touch of Hubris

Hamlet: Both
Good And Bad   City Ballet Not
                    For The Neophyte

Actors To Perform Cambodian Play

Speilberg's Vision: A Peripatetic Future

11) Concert review:
big words are manda-
tory.

12) Articles about stu-
dent productions usu-
ally have mixed re-
views.

13) Ballet review: big
words are mandatory.

14) Movie review: big
words are mandatory.

6) School papers love
to cover so-called mi-
nor sports.

5) Lately, much of
the sports page looks
like the business or
egal section.

Brothers

The Greeks

If all of college life were like that portrayed in "Animal House," then every guy would belong to a frat and every girl to a sorority. In reality, though some schools boast frat enrollment of as high as 85% of the total male population, the enrollments at most frats are considerably less than that and some schools have banned frats altogether.

In one way or another, you will probably be affected by frats or sororities, whether you become a full-fledged member or just drop by one of the parties for some free beer. Fraternities and sororities are as much a part of the college scene as books and pizza.

Whether there is any truth in the rumor that fraternities started when Aristotle got a bunch of Greeks together around a keg is irrelevant. What IS relevant is the Greek ideal of scholarly brotherhood upon which fraternities are based. A frater-nity is meant to be a place where the theories of the class-room can be given human qual-ities and placed into action. It should be a place where a group of men with the common bond of knowledge can share the ex-perience of maturity. And it should have a well-stocked bar.

Students join frats for differ-ent reasons. Maybe their dad was in one. Maybe they like the idea of being a member of an age-old tradition. Maybe they want to play on some really good IM teams. Maybe they just want to do what all of their friends are doing. At any rate, among the myriad of reasons for joining, one is bound to be for you.

The new candidates for the frat are looked over at frater-nity rush parties. At these par-ties you must drink wildly, re-member the names of key frat members, and appear to be having a good time all the while. It can be very difficult. The best thing to do is relax. Drop a few names or facts ("I was blowing chow when Nixon called me up

this morning to proofread his new book."), tell a few jokes (but avoid racist and ethnic ones; stick with sexist), or talk about sports ("How 'bout them Tigers?"). You'll do okay.

Joining a frat is a little more difficult than joining a record of the month club. You don't just put your name on the dotted line and wait for the good times; you have to earn your way in. This may mean a not-so-pleasant initiation, some not-so-legal hazings, or some not-so-moderate drinking. Most of these procedures are innocuous, but a few may leave lasting memories (like waking up in Arkansas in your underwear with only a dime and no way to get back to school in Oregon).

If you're a nerd, your chances of getting into a frat are fairly slim. Somehow it's hard to look cool at a luau with a calculator on your belt. But never fear. Some frats need nerds to keep up their GPA. Expect a room near the washers and dryers, though.

It should be noted that this brief summary of fraternities does not encompass the whole picture. Although fraternity members are known to cause havoc and make Dean Gerber look like a fool, they often perform many unheralded courtesies, such as walking old ladies across the street, or walking young ladies into their rooms.

Dean Gerber's Dilemma

Unlike "Animal House," very few dead horses are left in the Dean's office. Still, frats have a way of making their pranks seem more distinctive than those of other student groups. Dean Gerber has about had it with the Dekes. Examine the evidence, weigh the reasons for and against expulsion, and decide for yourself whether Dean Gerber should ban the Dekes.

Expulsion: Pro

1) Did a panty raid.*

2) Went carousing in car.**

3) During chem lecture, Professor Bernt pulled down screen; centerfold attached.

4) Disrupted halftime with projectiles from the stands.****

* Girls were still wearing panties.
** Stole a prof's Saab, crashed into the president's house, sunk car in lake.
*** Real Playmate under screen.
**** 200 rounds of 80mm mortar fire.

Expulsion: Con

No reasons.

The Trial: Initiation

Since hazings are no longer legal, fraternities have come up with a new method for heartily welcoming their new brothers: initiation. Many fraternity initiations have proven to be as colorful, mischievous, and hilarious as the hazings of the old days. Here are a few of the more common fraternity initiation rites.

A Brief Shopping Spree. Strip new members down to their jockeys, then send them to do the house's food shopping.

Fire and Ice. Set up relay races with new members in teams. The losing team must drink flaming shots of rum.

Grin and Bare It. Remove prospective members' clothes, then tie them to bannister in a sorority house.

Toxic Jocks. Make each new member down a six pack of beer. Strip the new members down to their jockeys and have them swim underwater across a pond of toxic chemical waste. When they return to the house, make them drink a fifth of vodka.

The Mercenary Position. Give pledges weapons and put them on military flights to Angola. Make them fight Communist forces for a week. When they return to the house, make them drink a fifth of vodka.

Brothers?

Joining a frat is a very personal decision which should not be taken lightly. As with any monumental dilemma in life, you should make a checklist weighing the advantages and disadvantages of your decision.

ADVANTAGES OF JOINING A FRAT

1) Good contacts with world-wide network of frat brothers.

2) Good way to meet girls. They always come to weekend frat functions.

3) Chance to learn how to treat fellow students with true feelings of brotherhood.

4) Many have nice houses.

5) They stress academics and have extensive test files and study aides which can be invaluable to learning the subject.

6) If you're not in one, you're a loser.

7) Your father and older brothers joined.

8) Guaranteed booze and good times.

DISADVANTAGES OF JOINING A FRAT

1) Forced to interact with other losers who were in the same frat.

2) No girls ever venture into a house full of sex-starved men during the week.

3) Learn that brotherhood does not exist.

4) Many have trashed houses.

5) They stress cheating and have extensive test files and study aides for keeping otherwise illiterates from flunking out.

6) If you're in one, you're a loser.

7) Your father and older brothers joined.

8) Guaranteed barfing and forced social situations.

Famous Frats

Obviously, fraternities are more popular at some schools than they are at others. Similarly, each fraternity differs from campus to campus. There are, however, some fraternities which have established a nation-wide reputation, and chances are you will eventually run into one or more of these. To help you in your search for a frat that's right for you, challenge your knowledge by matching the following frats with their descriptions below.

1) The oldest secret brotherhood in America. This frat is very popular in the South, and often receives a lot of flak for flying Confederate colors above the American flag.

2) Boasts over 151 chapters nationwide. Fraternity magazine was first of its kind, and has a circulation of 98,000, largest among the frat publications. Good reputation.

3) Another famous nationwide fraternity. Assets in excess of $1,500,000. Over 115,000 initiates. John Wayne was one.

4) Pompous British fraternity famous for artistic productions of obscure plays. Very popular with upper-class intellectuals who think this is the ultimate in culture. They forget that while the actors are drinking tea in the garden, the actual country is being flushed down the toilet.

5) Mostly Black fraternity. In serious financial trouble because of overpayment of intramural athletes, and the fact that people will no longer pay exhorbitant prices to get into their parties.

a) NBA
b) BBC
c) SAE
d) Sigma Chi
e) KA

Answers: 1e; 2c; 3d; 4b; 5a.

Sisters

If you're thinking about joining a sorority, you probably know by now that most of the advantage of "sisterhood" is the great social calendar.

Mixers. Mixers are often the attraction of sororities seeking light socializing under the guise of getting tipsy. If the idea behind mixers seems simple and shallow, then you'll have no problem understanding why the conversation will remind you of a Glory Rug Cleaner commercial. If you expect to find everyone hovered around the mpunch bowl and only the most superficial girls making the first moves, you're not in for a big surprise. Mixers are usually low key and casual, so wear your best gown and heels.

As you can imagine, mixers aren't for everyone. Specifically, they're not for the shy, the

introspective, the inhibited, the deep-thinking, or the oversexed. In addition, some men feel imported, much like cattle or Corollas. If the mixer is held at the sorority house or on campus at your all girls' school, remember that you have home turf advantage. This means being able to leave whenever you want.

Little Sisters and Big Brothers. The origins of the Little Sisters and Big Brothers scene also lie buried in the ancient Greek circle. Unaffiliated girls, usually freshpersons, or sorority members become "Little Sisters" to their "Big Brothers," meaning associated frat guys. The relationship is Brady Bunch-like in appearance, though many have wondered just how platonic these get. To the satisfaction of non-Greeks and the frustration of fraternities, the link rarely becomes incestual and more often serves to fill the female void not found in a coed environment.

To keep the Little Sisters and

Changing Tastes
Magazine Subscriptions Over the Years

Freshmen year: Seventeen

Sophomore Year: Glamour

Junior Year: Cosmospolitan

Senior Year: Bride

Big Brothers in place, some of the more progressive universities have devised an "Ugly Mothers" program which oversees the other two. First conceived by a group of retired grammar school cafeteria supervisors, the Ugly Mothers hang around frat or sorority houses cleaning, going into tirades, and nagging Big Brothers with exhortations like, "Joel, why don't you take your little sister to the frat party tonight?" Frat guys respond with "Oh Mom, do I have to?" only to be pelted with a "Damn it, Joel,

---

Escorts For The Formal

GOOD CHOICES

1) Son of professor.
2) Son of famous alumnus.
3) Son of US Representative.
4) Son of US Senator.
5) Son of US President.

BAD CHOICES

1) Son of grad student.
2) Son of president of Uganda.
3) Son of shoe salesman.
4) Son of lingerie salesman.
5) Son of Sam.

This year's letter to new members.

Hi! Hi! Hi ! ! ! ! ! ! ! ! !

This year's officers, Jenny, Maura, and I want to welcome you, our special new member of Kappa Epsilon Pi. We're so excited about this year, especially since the new READING ROOM is to be added to our house. We just know that you must be excited too.

Since we're alsways so excited, it's easy to forget to tell you some things you'll need to know. One of the purposes of this letter is to remind you of the Kappa "Codes to Live By."

1) Kappa is best and we are all lucky to be members.
2) All kappas pledge to treat everyone equally, including minorities or people who don't wash their hair regularly.
3) It is an age-old tradition for Kappas to keep up with the times.
4) Kappas do not get drunk or tipsy, except on champagne or punch.
5) We must always stay together and cherish our sisterhood forever and ever.

We just know that you love Kappa enough to obey these rules, because if you don't obey them you'll receive the worst punishment of all; expulsion from Kappa. The very thought makes me shudder! ! !

We just know that we'll have so much fun and be best friends for life this year. We can't wait to see all of you again.

Yours in Kappa,

Alycia Landsdale

Alycia Landsdale,
Kappa Recording Secretary

YES! for the fourteenth time, and stop playing with that tennis racket before you poke someone's eye out!" Still other colleges report designs for a Fathers program as yet on the drawing board.

Dates for the Formal. As an ostentatious gesture of social eloquence, each sorority plans a formal, often in the early spring. After all the arrange-ments have been made, the reservations confirmed, the invitations mailed, and the dresses purchased (solely for that occasion), the question of whom to ask still haunts a few girls. The essence of the choice, of course, is whether you want a mere escort or you dream of cultivating the opportunity into a prospective romance. Most pick a mere escort.

Wide World of College Sports

Even if you're not a sports fan you cannot deny the popularity of college athletics. While each college's sports program differs in scope and intensity, there is an excellent chance that your college has some sort of athletics. Whether it's Ohio State or Ohio Wesleyan, the fact remains that sports play an important role in campus life.

Varsity sports exist for a number of reasons. To the student athlete, sports are a chance to further one's skills in a particular area, enjoy the camaraderie of a team, and, in some cases, prepare for a career in professional sports. To the college, athletics can bring prestige, as well as a great deal of money. To the student body,

Photo courtesy Stanford University

athletics provide another form of campus entertainment. Finally, to the alumni, sports provide an excuse to get drunk in public and wear leisure suits in school colors.

At some colleges, athletics are heavily emphasized, and in many cases seem to be the university's main concern. These places often have separate dormitories for the athletes, who are rarely seen around campus except at game time. While this does make the division between athletes and non-athletes greater, it also provides employment to area youngsters who pick up spare bucks by selling "Maps to Stars' Rooms" and by cleaning dirty cleats.

Come game time, all this seems trivial. When you're chugging your eighth beer and passing your buddy's girlfriend up the stadium rows while you're football team clobbers its arch-rival, or vacationing in New Orleans while your team plays in the NCAA basketball championships, you couldn't care less if the star player got an F in remedial English 1. You're happy, you're partying, and he helped you get to that state of mind. Indeed, college sports have something for everyone.

Spectator sports are exciting events, but if you are at all athletically-inclined, you will undoubtedly feel the need to participate in some athletic events yourself. Here's where intramurals come into the pic-

ture. Intramurals have something to offer everyone, whether you're a first-time water polo hacker or an ex- all-state basketball stud. The best thing about intramurals is the lack of the "win-at-all-costs" philosophy. There will be some serious athletes, but you won't run into any Bobby Knight types; you're pretty much on your own. While you're at it, make sure you give your team a creative name. Forget "Lions" and "Tigers" and "Bears"; you're in college. Call your team the "PLO" or the "Soviet Union" and watch people cringe.

Not everyone desires to be an intramural athlete, but even those anti-jock types will run into athletics in various collegiate settings. If you live in a dorm, you'll encounter numerous competitions in the course of a normal school year. Drunken obstacle courses around the dorm lounge can be as challenging as any soccer match, and few golf shots are as tough as maneuvering a potential sex partner into your cramped room while your roommate snoozes away.

When you think about it, nearly every aspect of college can be related to sports, the grading system being one of college life's greatest games. Whether you're a Rose Bowl quarterback or someone whose only athletic ability involves unscrewing a light bulb, you're part of the college athletic scene.

Spectatorless Sports

The problem with high school perennials like football or basketball is you just can't even dream of joining the team unless you're Superman. Today you may be captain of the football team and dating the head cheerleader; tomorrow you'll realize that joining the university squad would be as unrealistic as playing for the Miami Dolphins. Still, you want to play, and intramural sports just aren't attractive enough. What's called for here is a little research.

The truth is that there are many other sports screaming for you to pick up the raquet, stick, or ball. Sometimes you find yourself in an ego crisis; you've never thought of yourself as anything other than a hooper or a gridiron man. Soon you'll get over it, though, and you'll find the "obscure" sports just as exciting.

Lacrosse. Originally played by the American Indian, this sport is both stylish and tough, which makes it a great substitute for football. So what if nobody comes to see the games? Everybody in the dorm will know you're on the team when you walk around wearing the uniform and beautifully stick-handling balls, apples, and grapefruit in the lounge. Violent? It sure is, and dormmates will realize this when they see all the protective wear needed.

Squash. Usually a very low key sport, squash is perfect for the Porsche set. This type of athlete likes to work up a sweat (known as "perspiration"), but doesn't like getting his or her fingernails dirty. Some of the advantages include being able to stroll to the side of the court for a quick drink between sets and being able to hold a conversation with your partner. Usual topics of conversation are:

—where to get Polo shirts at half price
—problems with romance
—broker's advice

Racquetball (poor man's squash). A ball bounces around a small room and the players chase it frantically, attempting to take our their aggressions. There is very little similarity with basketball (in which a large ball bounces around a large room and the players chase it frantically). Some disciples point out the symbolism of the game (the ball representing the meaning of life and the players vainly in pursuit) while others just carry the racquet around and play with balls, apples, and grapefruit.

Rugby. Although British in invention, rugby is gaining popularity on American college campuses and the team frequently departs for such exotic lands as New Zealand. Obviously, this is a great sport; if nothing else you'll get a shirt out of it, and these to be very fashionable and expensive. Although potentially dangerous to the human health, you don't have to do much except move around with a large heap of human flesh and get muddy. It's clearly not football or else people would come to watch the games, but everyone will think you're almost as tough.

Water Polo. If you don't play this already and haven't been training since you were a Californian infant, forget it. The only way your friends could tell if you were playing water polo would be by your green hair or your ubiquitous presence in warm-ups. Besides, you'd really have to work out and who wants that?

Cycling. Cycling has become very popular in the last decade, partly due to the success of the movie Breaking Away. It is very expensive, however, and requires a lot of time devoted to mechanics and training. If you start today and force yourself to ride every day, you just might make it to the Tour de France in about ten years.

Skiing. If you live near mountains, there's probably snow, and that means one thing: skiing. Many students select colleges by ski potential and some students even try to study a little while on ski trips. Skiing has some things in common with cycling; you have to be reasonably well off to partake heavily in the sport, and unless you've been at it a long time, you'll

never be able to compete with the real pros.

Cricket, Martial Arts, Bowling. Are these really sports?

Polo. Contrary to popular belief, the shirt is not a prerequisite for the game. In addition, most people have come to believe that polo is an elitist sport intended strictly for the rich and that very few players are actually good. They're right.

Surfing. Promoted chiefly by California and Hawaii, surfing has not caught on in other states such as Tennessee and South Dakota. *Awesome* is the word for surfing, but is it veritably a sport? Surfing is rarely seen other than on T.V. - either on ABC Wide World of Sports or in *Frankie & Annette Hang Ten on the Wild Side.* Learn the jargon and move to the coast, but be forewarned that surfing in no way resembles either football or basketball.

Ultimate Frisbee. This relatively new sport is often played by burnouts and druggies, though the action would imply intense physical ability required. This leads us to examine the seriousness of the sport. NCAA Ultimate Frisbee Championships on national television replacing football? Crowds of 30,000 assembled in Schaeffer Stadium to watch a glorified pie plate fly around? Not quite. The word *Ultimate* tells us something here; why not *Awesome* Frisbee, or Frisbee *Max*? Why isn't there Ultimate Baseball, or Soccer Ultimatum? It may not be a major sport, but if your college doesn't have an Ultimate Frisbee team, maybe it hasn't heard of the 20th century.

Take a Seat

College football games are usually pretty big events. Even if your school has a losing record, you can have fun talking with friends or drowning your sorrows in alcohol. As a result, demand for good seating in the stadium is usually high.

At many schools, if you don't arrive at the stadium before 9:00 am on the day of the game, you won't get a decent seat. If you arrive late, you'll want to know where to sit and where not to sit. Use this stadium guide to decide which seats will be open, which will be taken, and which will not be suitable.

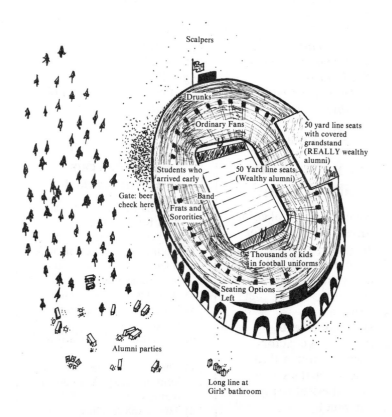

Scalpers

Drunks

Ordinary Fans

50 yard line seats with covered grandstand (REALLY wealthy alumni)

Students who arrived early

50 Yard line seats (Wealthy alumni)

Gate: beer check here

Band

Frats and Sororities

Thousands of kids in football uniforms

Seating Options Left

Alumni parties

Long line at Girls' bathroom

Bowling

In recent years, the number of post-season college football bowl games has increased drastically. While this has given more universities the chance to participate in post-season play, it has also provided the student sports fan with a considerable challenge: trying to keep track of obscure bowls in obscure cities.

Try to match the bowl game with the city in which it is played. Some are obvious, some are obscure, some are facetious.

1. *Cotton Bowl*
2. *Sugar Bowl*
3. *Peach Bowl*
4. *Bean Bowl*
5. *Independence Bowl*
6. *Unemployment Bowl*
7. *Fiesta Bowl*
8. *Orange Bowl*
9. *Obscure Bowl*

a. New Orleans, Louisiana
b. Freeport, Maine
c. Tempe, Arizona
d. Shreveport, Louisiana
e. White House
f. Atlanta, Georgia
g. Miami, Florida
h. Obscureville, Nevada
i. Dallas, Texas

Answers:
1-i,2-a,3-f,4-b,5-d,6-e,7-c,8-g,9-h.

How to Root Like Alumni

1. Wear only school colors.
2. Have a tailgater before the game.
3. Do old school yells and songs that no one knows anymore.
4. Drink a lot.
5. Sit in good seats.
6. Have a huge victory celebration in a local hotel after the game (regardless of the game's outcome).

How To Tell If Your Team Is Not Ranked

1) During the game the fans root for the other team.
2) Tickets to games are cheap.
3) Your school is not mentioned on the Prudential College Scoreboard.
4) Athletes get good grades.
5) You study during home games.
6) The Alumni Association is small.
7) There is a special news bulletin on local TV when the teams wins.
8) The coach teaches.

FIVE

SOCIAL SCIENCES

PARTYING AT COLLEGE

A party is to the college student what Miller Time is to the dock worker. It is a place where you can get down, get funky, and then get back up again. After a hard week studying, writing papers, and pursuing other intellectual venues, you need a chance to let off steam and take it easy with your friends. Partying is the way to do this. Though different groups have different ways of partying, most parties contain similar ingredients: *drinking, dancing,* and *socializing.*

Drinking

Drinking at a party is essential. Drinks have a way of legitimizing otherwise unacceptable social activity. "Hey, what the hell is John doing flopping on the ground like that?" "He's had twelve beers." "Oh. For a minute there I thought something was wrong."

If drinks are for relaxation at one end of the spectrum, then at the other end they are for getting one blasted out of one's mind. To this end, beer bongs, drinking games, and punch spiked with pure grain alcohol have been invented. For those who choose to abstain, many good party hosts provide non-alcoholic alternatives, usually six or seven cans of Shasta Creme

Soda located next to and sometimes in the trash can.

Dancing

Dancing, like drinking, removes inhibition, loosens you up, and gets you to do things that you otherwise might not do. The stereo will blare the sounds of Boston, AC/DC, and The Doobie Brothers (all impossible to dance to). When "China Grove" starts up, find a partner and head out to the dance floor.

The problem of how to combine the spontaneity of free dancing with the uniformity of contact dancing has plagued partiers for years. Fortunately, some of the more preppy institutions have arrived at what they consider a solution: *gatoring*. This famous dance step involves half sexual, half epileptic writhing on the floor to the wild beat of the music. Whether or not the dance was derived from the emblem on preppy clothing is unclear, but it is known that at several less prestigious and less label-conscious universities, the "fox" is becoming the party dance.

Generally, you can get by on the dance floor if you just have a rudimentary sense of rhythm. If you know certain techniques, like raising your arms up a lot on Stones' songs, and shuffling your feet during a Michael Jackson ditty, you should do just fine. If you have the mis-

fortune of being a good dancer and your partner is a walrus, just remember that most songs are only three or four minutes long. Break away by saying, "Whoa! That tired me out. I'd better get something to drink."

Socializing

A party is a good way to get to know people. You are removed from your everyday environment and placed into an atmosphere of good times set to incredibly loud music. To begin, you should know some unusual and provocative questions to go with the standard "What's your name? What's your major? Where are you from?" Try "Do anchovies make you barf?"

Unfortunately, you will not always be enraptured by everyone you meet at parties. Sometimes you will find yourself discussing stupid things with a boring person. One good way to get out of a situation like this is to say "Do you have any intelligent, good looking friends?" or "Boy, am I glad that I'm almost over the plague."

Parties are great. They give you a chance to do things you normally wouldn't. Drink it up. Dance. Meet people. Don't worry if you can't always get into the party scene. You can always go back to your room, put on a record, and write a friend about how you hate parties.

How Do You Party?

Lots of college students profess to be partiers, but not so many can actually stand up to their self-awarded reputation. Not everyone is willing to gator when the floor is soaked in beer, to drink when there is nothing left but pure grain alcohol, or to pass out at a wine and cheese hour with a professor. But some people are. They're the true partiers. Find out what kind of a partier you are by taking this simple test.

1) What's your favorite beverage?
2) What do you wear on your head while partying?
3) How late do your parties last?
4) When do you throw a party?
5) Who is the last guest at your parties?
6) Name your favorite dance step.

How You Responded:

1) *Milk.* If you wrote this, then you'd better think about spending another year in high school.
Beer. Good. No doubt you're in college.
Drano. Now that's more like it. So far you're on the road to party paradise.

2) *Bryl Creem.* Funny, very funny.
Baseball cap. Not bad. At least people will think you're an athlete.
Lampshade. George Jetson would be proud of you.

3) *12 a.m.* Have you considered working for "Welcome Wagon?"
3:00 a.m. Better. Just late enough to insure that you'll sleep through classes.
Into Your Next Year. Are you the most popular person on campus?

4) *Only on Christmas or other holidays.* Do you remember to leave milk and cookies for Santa, too?
Weekend with nothing else going on. It's better than studying.
If the sun comes up. This puts you in the "Party Monster" category.

5) *You.* Does anyone else come?
Your girlfriend or boyfriend. Cute. At least they're loyal.
Rod Stewart. Are YOU Rod Stewart?

6) *Disco.* What? These are the eighties!
Gator. Pretty wild, but smells up your clothes.
Coma. Now you're a partier.

Read Between The Lines

Campus parties come in all shapes and sizes. Some are fantastic. Others are disastrous.

Part of your indoctrination during your four years at college will be learning to understand

* STUDENT-SPONSORED PARTIES *

Grad Student Party

Poster stresses assets, especially those which appeal to undergraduates (beer, music). It doesn't mention the fact that there will be hundreds of nerds, foreigners, and people whose idea of fun is discussing Boyle's Law and Fibonacci numbers for three hours.

Attracts:

Nerds, foreigners, people whose idea of fun is discussing Boyle's Law and Fibonacci numbers for three hours.

Dormitory Party

Usually involves a gimmick or two to try and entice outsiders to the party. Despite these attempts, party is still same old crowd doing same old things.

Attracts:

Some members of the dorm, a couple of curious passers-by, middle east war mongers.

party advertisements. As a freshman, if you see a poster advertising a "huge blowout party in the Medieval Mathematics department" you'll probably go and be disappointed when you see eleven people sitting around, drinking mead, and discussing Medieval Mathematics. By the time you get to be a senior, though, you'll recognize that type of poster as the sign of a terrible party, and you'll avoid the whole thing. Take a look at some of these posters, and try to figure out what the real story is.

Popular Fraternity Party

This frat doesn't even need advertising for its parties. Word has already spread around campus by noon the preceding day.

Attracts:

Ninety percent of campus.

Off Campus Party

Given by group of three or four who live off campus. Ugly poster. Map takes up half the street and is readable only to experienced orienteers or Lewis and Clark.

Attracts:

A few close friends of the hosts. Lewis and Clark.

* UNIVERSITY-SPONSORED PARTIES *

Department

If you go expecting a group of intellectual profs discussing Donne and Milton, you're in for a shock. More likely you'll find drunk intellectual profs blabbering about Donne and Milton.

Speakers' Bureau

Despite brilliant panel, university still feels the need to try to tempt more students with beer and music. Turns "Meet the Nation" into "Woodstock III."

What's the Difference?

1) *Sherry/Wine.* Very mellow social situation. Probably a gathering with a member of the faculty or administration. Avoid saying words like "fart" or "condom."

2) *Dacquiries.* A spontaneous activity with other members of the dorm. Laugh a lot and say you heard someone saying "fart" or "condom" at a sherry hour which you attended.

3) *Beer.* Big party with loud music and many drunk people. Every other word should be "fart" or "condom."

4) *Spiked punch.* Formal party where no one is supposed to get drunk so everyone does. Fart a lot and have a supply of condoms.

Is It A Party?

In college, the word "party" is used to label nearly every kind of social gathering, no matter what the size or function. There's a need for a more exact definition of various bashes. Each type has its own atmosphere and its own requirements.

GET TOGETHER

Number of people:
  4-10.
Where held:
  Dorm room.
What to bring:
  Snacks, six pack of Lowenbrau.
What happens:
  Share memories and laughter with close friends, discuss future plans, get semi-drunk, and decide to go bowling as a joke.

GATHERING

Number of people:
  10-20.
Where held:
  Someone's house.
What to bring:
  Covered dish, wine.
What happens:
  Talk about classes, majors, world problems; a rather mellow evening with most people leaving around 11:00; a few hardcores stay later to discuss the effects of Canada's new economic policy.

PARTY

Number of people:
  20-150
Where held:
  Dorm, sorority house.
What to bring:
  Sense of humor, beer mug, virginity.
What happens:
  Drinking, dancing, and socializing.

EVENT

Number of people:
  150-12,000.
Where held:
  Frat, arena.
What to bring:
  Date, funny hat.
What happens:
  Lose date and spend entire time trying to find him or her while getting drunk and running into people you don't care to see.

MOB SCENE

Number of people:
  12,000-55,000.
Where held:
  Football stadium, Times Square.
What to bring:
  Flask of liquor, pennants.
What happens:
  Spend time talking to friends, run into people you know from campus, and pay attention to anything but what you're actually there for.

COUP D'ETAT

Number of people:
  55,000-1,200,000.
Where held:
  Insignificant South American country.
What to bring:
  Submachine gun, grenades, copy of *How to Run Your Own Country.*
What happens:
  Get rowdy, burn leader in effigy, capture leader, burn him in reality, and shout "Down with imperialist American dogs!"

A Beginner's Guide To The Drinks

By now you should realize that drinking is imperative at college. At a party, you can't stand around trying to make conversation without a drink. First of all, everyone around you will be drinking, and without a drink in your hand you just don't fit in.

Too often inexperienced drinkers bow to this social pressure by drinking huge amounts and later regretting it. You can't learn to be a big drinker overnight, but you can learn how to look like a wild partier even though you're not Dean Martin.

Dacquiries. Watch out! These are very dangerous for the inexperienced drinker. Because they taste great, you may forget that they're alcoholic. Provided you use good judgment, dacquiries are a tasty alternative for the beginner.

Beer. Besides being the staple of the college drinker, beer can be great for the beginner because you probably hate the taste and won't drink it. It's easy to carry the same beer cup around all night. (For more on beer, see facing page.)

Punch. If you're at a party which provides punch as a non-alcoholic alternative, be extra careful that it's not spiked with PGA (pure grain alcohol). PGA punch compares to a dacquiri as an atomic bomb does to a stick of dynamite. The purpose of punch is not to quench your thirst. Your best bet is to stay away and just act drunk.

Wine. Always a great choice for inexperienced drinkers, wine automatically raises your IQ 50 points. You can sip it because its purpose is to loosen you up rather than to get you drunk. Unfortunately, you won't find wine at too many keg parties.

Mixed drinks. If you know the bartender, then you're in business. Order a scotch and water on the rocks with extra water. Mixed drinks are sipped even more slowly than wine, so as long as you act cool, you should be fine.

Champagne. If you're a girl, STAY AWAY. After one glass you'll be giggling and after a few more you'll be hitchiking to San Jose with the janitor.

The Beer Facts

Serious beer drinkers know all about beer drinking. Teetotalers don't need to know anything. But what about the student who falls in between those two catgories? Should you pass up a positive social situation because you don't know anything about beer drinking etiquette? Or should you go ahead and fake it, risking discovery of your lack of knowlege?

Needless to say, neither of the previous solutions is a viable one. The best way to enjoy a beer-laden social life is to memorize a few simple facts and methods, thus avoiding any embarrassment or regret.

Type of Container	Group Situation	Alone
Shot Glass	Drinking Games	Solitary Drinkers
Can/Bottle	Thirst Quencher	Light Drinkers
Six-Pack	Social Drinking	Cruising in Cars
Case	Impromptu Party	Serious Drinkers
Pony Keg	Medium-Sized Parties	REALLY Serious Drinkers
Half Keg (Keg)	Large Parties	Frat Members

Games People Play

Drinking can become fairly routine after a few wild college parties, so students are constantly looking for ways to enliven the drinking atmosphere. One solution is drinking games. By making an ordinary night of imbibing into a contest, you'll be able to get drunk without the fear of boredom.

1) Thumper

What you need:
10-20 people and several cases of wine or beer.
Where held:
Dorm lounge around big table.
How to play:
Each person has signal; game progresses around table by responding to signal. If you miss a signal or make an error in etiquette, you must take a drink.
How to win:
Know your signal. Caution: don't play with pros; they're cruel.
Object:
Get drunk.

2) Quarters

What you need:
5-15 people, several cases of beer, mugs, and quarters.
Where held:
Dorm room or campus pub.
How to play:
Try to bounce quarters into people's mugs. If the quarter lands in the mug, the owner must drink. (Caution: in advanced stages of this game, some people imbibe everything in their mug, including the quarter.)
How to win:
Stay sober. Hint: use small mug with lid top.
Object:
Get drunk.

3) Blow Pong

What you need:
15-20 people, keg of beer, and ping pong ball and table.
Where held:
Anywhere you can find a ping pong table.
How to play:

Two teams kneeling at the opposite ends of the table. One team tries to blow a ping pong ball over the heads of the other team. If the first team is successful, the second team must drink.

How to win:

Each successful try is worth a point. First team to 21 wins. (Caution: easy to hyperventilate and pass out.)

Object:

Get drunk.

4) Get the Girls Drunk

What you need:

10 guys, 10 girls, several cases of beer, and some gimmick.

Where held:

One of the guy's rooms.

How to play:

Under the pretense of a trivial game, guys casually fill the empty glasses of the girls. Continue until girls pass out.

How to win:

Don't play.

Object:

No one is quite sure.

Easy Method to "Shot-Gunning" a Beer

1) With can opener, put hole in side or bottom of can.

2) Hold beer over head, mouth over hole. Pop top and guzzle. Don't choke.

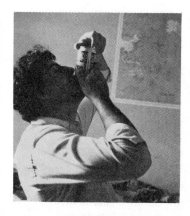

3) Dispose of properly.

Faking It

If you attend college in a state where the legal drinking age is over eighteen, you will find yourself in need of a fake I.D. which will enable you to buy alcoholic beverages, both at bars and liquor stores.

Throughout the years, students have tried countless ways to beat the law. Some are good. Some are bad.

Worst Ways

1) Borrow someone else's I.D. Note: make sure this person looks like you. If not, you could be up against a forgery charge.

3) Have a campus con-man make a fake driver's license for you. Usually has a mistake or two on it, and ends up looking like a meal card.

Best Ways

1) Be of legal age.

2) Get a duplicate license from a friend of legal age who lives in another state.

3) Don't drink.

2) Send away for a fake I.D. For $25 you get a cheap-looking card from an obscure state, which has a fake-sounding address and says, *Not a valid license.*

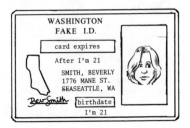

Altered States

While the use of so-called "recreational drugs" has declined in the past few years, there's still a good chance that you'll encounter drugs in one way or another during your college years. Through the decades, use of various drugs has created certain mystiques, and without attempting to influence anyone's lifestyle, we urge you to use discretion in particular social situations; if not . . .

MARIJUANA . . .in dorm room with a group of people.

What You Think Will Happen. You'll get an incredible head rush. You'll realize that the secret of life is simple and attainable. You'll have incredible conversations with other students. You'll settle down in a warm bed for a good night's sleep.

What Actually Happens. You get an incredible headache. You realize that life is screwed up and your existence is meaningless. You cannot relate to anyone else. You leave the room and order pizza to satiate an extreme hunger. You sack out on a hard, cold cement floor.

COCAINE. . . on a date.

What You Think Will Happen. You'll get a tingling, euphoric feeling in your throat, nose and head. You'll feel very sensual and excited. You'll drive to a romantic spot in the foothills and make wild, passionate love. You'll wake up in your partner's arms.

What Actually Happens. You get a sore throat and a runny nose. You become amazingly horny and hyperactive. You drive to a romantic spot in the foothills and run the car into a ditch. You wake up in the hospital.

AMPHETAMINES (SPEED) . . .at a dorm party.

What You Think Will Happen. You'll be energetic and spontaneous. You'll bop all over the dance floor to the cheers of your dormmates. You'll hit it off with an attractive member of the opposite sex. You're eyed jealously as you head back to your room for some more fun.

What Actually Happens. You're obnoxious and predictable. You crash around on the dance floor to the jeers and glares of your doormmates. You utter unintelligible gibberish to an attractive member of the opposite sex. You're dismissed as "rude and drunk" as you stumble back to your room alone and try to sleep.

Caution:
Men Prowling

The "pickup scene" at a college party can be both a boon and a bane to you, the collegiate woman. On one hand, you have your mother telling you how she met your father for the first time at a Beta Theta Pi party, while at the same time your aunt is claiming that she still gets obscene phone calls from some loon she met at the same party.

Be forewarned that college parties bring out the extremes of both worlds; you'll meet some great people, but you'll also meet some of the biggest losers of all time. In this section, you'll get a brief glimpse of some different types of guys you'll probably meet at a campus fete. Some are dangerous and some are innocuous, but all will be looking at you, so it's in your best interests that you peruse this Guide to Party Types.

Not Threats

1) **The Nerd.** He's the model for those "Are you a Nerd?" posters you see in stores. God only knows why he's even at the party in the first place. He doesn't know what sex is, and is only a threat if YOU ask HIM to dance. DON'T . . . unless you REALLY need the answer to #8 on the Physics problem set.

2) **The Apathetic Partier.** Lives by the keg. If you happen to wander into his domain, he'll probably make a lewd comment or suggestion, but don't worry; he's too drunk to try anything. Besides, filling up your beer is the closest thing to sex he's had in a long time.

3) **The Gagster.** When everyone else is trying their best to look nice, he's wearing army pants, a UVA T-shirt and a hat. He may ask you to dance, but he won't try to pick you up because to him, getting a laugh is more important than getting a girlfriend.

4) **The Gay.** Obviously.

The Successful Scammer

Looks/Dress. Inevitably the best-looking guy at the party. Surprisingly casual in his dress, since he knows his great looks can carry him in any situation.

Where Found at Party. NEVER dancing. Always on the perimeter of the dance floor, eyes flashing left to right, checking out the scene. Usually alone, although he may be with a scamming buddy.

Personality/Characteristics. Smooth talker, yet doesn't have to resort to cliches. Chances are he'll probably already know who you are even though he won't let on. Usually a frat man, his room comes equipped with dimmer switch, waterbed, and guest book (make sure you sign in).

How to Avoid.

a) Dance a lot.
b) Stay in a large group of friends.
c) Keep convincing yourself that good looks aren't everything.

SAMPLE PARTY CONVERSATION

He: *"You were in my biology class last quarter, weren't you?"*
She: *"No."*
He: *"Oh, I'm sorry. Well, how's this party, anyway? I just got here."*
She: *"Uh, it's okay."*
He: *"Well, the party next door is really hopping. Wanna go check it out?"*

The Unsuccessful Scammer

How to Avoid.

a) Dance a lot.
b) Never believe a thing he says.
c) Introduce him to an acquaintance who WILL believe him.

Looks/Dress. Also very good-looking, but dress usually gives him away because he tries too hard. Usually overdressed, and more often than not, he has a gold chain the size of a hula hoop around his neck.

Where Found at Party. On the outskirts of the dance floor like the Successful Scammer, but his eye contact is much more obvious and blatant.

Personality/Characteristics. Overbearing personality oozing decadence (drugs are often a part of his pitch) and deceit. He'll use cliches, insincerities, and even lies. Room looks like a bachelor pad from an X-rated movie.

SAMPLE PARTY CONVERSATION

He: *"Don't I know you from somewhere?*

She: *"I don't think so."*

He: *"Yeah, I do. I got it . . . biology class. You were the best-looking girl in there."*

She: *"I never took Bio."*

He: *"Well, that's okay with me. Wanna go check out my room? We could do a couple of lines and talk about life or something."*

The Ego-Gratifying Dancing King

Looks/Dress. Good-looking and he knows it. Lots of eyebrow action. Well-dressed yet with a touch of cockiness added by something extraneous like a bandanna or a brim hat.

Where Found at Party. Dancing. Every dance, and with a different girl each time. Even dances to "Free Bird."

Personality/Characteristics. Self-confident and self-centered. Has to dance so everyone will see him. Only reason he tries to pick up on you is so others will think he's a real ladies man. One eye in nearest mirror.

How to Avoid.

a) Don't dance at all.
b) Deflate his ego by asking if he's from the local high
c) school.
Mention your psychotic 6'6" boyfriend on the football team who just went to get a beer.

SAMPLE PARTY
CONVERSATION

He: *"Hi. You weren't in my Bio, were you? No, you weren't. Wanna dance with me?"*

She: *"Not really. I'm leaving soon."*

He: *"Aw, c'mon babe. Only one dance, it'll do you good."*

She: *"No, thank you."*

He: *"All right, but you don't know what you're missing. Twenty-five other chicks can't be wrong."*

The Boring Nice Guy

How to Avoid.

a) Act uninterested.
b) Scare him off by mentioning how much cocaine and acid you've done.
c) Yawn and say you have to go wash your hair.

Looks/Dress. Average looks. Always clean cut. Often very preppily dressed.

Where Found at Party. Walking around a lot, looking for friends or potential dance partners. Often travels in groups.

Personality/Characteristics. He's sincere. He's honest. He's nice. He's polite. He's concerned. But . . . HE'S BORING AS HELL.

SAMPLE PARTY CONVERSATION

He: *"Hi"*
She: *"Hi."*
He: *"I'm Richie. Weren't you in my Biology class?"*
She: *"No."*
He: *"Oh. How 'bout them 'Dawgs?"*
She: *"Yeah, that was a great game."*
He: *"Want to dance?"*
She: *"No, thanks. I'll be leaving soon."*
He: *"Okay. Well, nice talking to you. Bye."*

The God Squadder

Looks/Dress. Extremely clean-cut and usually fairly good-looking. Probably has an article of "fad" clothing on to show how he can "relate" to the college scene.

Where Found at Party. All over. Talking to anybody who will listen.

Personality/Characteristics. Friendly, talkative, and interesting, until he gets around to religion. Then it's all over. Has read *How to Pick Up Girls For Christ* fifteen times.

SAMPLE PARTY CONVERSATION

He: *"Hi, how's it going? Did you ever take Bio?"*

She: *"No, I didn't."*

He: *"I'm sorry. Well, how's life?"*

She: *"Oh, not bad. Okay, I guess."*

He: *"What's wrong?"*

She: *"I've just got so much work to do."*

He: *"Do you realize that Jesus can help you with that work?"*

She: *"What does he know about Marine Ecology?"*

He: *"Everything. Would you like to get together and talk about this some time?"*

How to Avoid.

a) Offer him a drink.
b) Excuse yourself to "go get high."
c) Tell him that you're already saved and jump out onto the dance floor.

Party Girls

Certain rules and regulations of the pick-up scene can be applied to the collegiate male. In high school, picking up (if it existed) was most likely spontaneous, whimsical, and not too difficult. Those memories should be stored with your yearbook and diploma, because in college things will probably be a lot different.

In nearly all cases the traditional "singles-bar" approach employed by those ostentatious guys in leisure suits and gold chains simply will not work with mature and sophisticated college women. Save that method until you feel your first midlife crisis coming on.

What you need to do is become aware of certain people and certain situations in order to facilitate your chances of meeting someone with whom you can be compatible. Since college is a completely different ball game, you should know some of the players and most of the rules.

THE OBJECT

The object of the pick-up is the single most important principle in the game. Looks and personality are essential, although some people subscribe to the "any port in a storm" adage.

You may experience a deeply meaningful encounter with someone and feel compelled to marry her on the spot. If not, there's always the one night stand. Since marriage probably isn't one of your first priorities, the latter scenario is the one you'll need to know about.

In the course of a collegiate night of partying, you may run into one or more of these women. You'll probably marry someone who's not on this list.

1) **The Maybelline Queen.** Remember high school? This is a "high school chick" who has undergone the trauma of graduation. Often wearing a pair of undersized Calvin Klein jeans and carrying a purse, the Maybelline Queen does not attend college, but instead works in a hair cutting salon or a department store. Travels in herds.

2) **The Phony.** A physiological enigma. Somehow, this girl manages to have five faces instead of the usual one. Believes that she is everyone's best friend, and will pretend to be interested in your stamp collection while eyeing the star quarterback across the room. Throws

out catchy phrases like "Call me next week, promise? You'd better!" Mysteriously never home.

3) **The Nymphomaniac.** An extinct or dying breed on most campuses, with the exception of several California schools. If she exists at your college, don't worry; you'll never see her.

4) **The Holy Roller.** Not to be confused with the High Roller. A WASP version of the good Catholic girls Billy Joel used to sing about. Though often incredibly beautiful, she's a guaranteed rejection. If you think you are going to run off to her Bible study class to score some points, forget it. Her boyfriend is probably a campus stud anyway.

5) **The Local High Schooler.** A younger version of the "Maybelline Queen." She is only at the frat party for one reason,

and it's not to learn Spanish. Try not to let your friends see you with her, and NEVER tell her your real name. Two midterms, a paper, and a statutory rape trial make for a tough week.

6) **The Intellectual.** Watch out for this one. You'll tell her you've got to finish Hamlet tomorrow and she'll berate you for stopping somewhere in the

middle. You've read *The Sun Also Rises* for Freshman English; her father was a personal friend of Hemingway. Never discuss books, and don't throw out an opinion concerning the lone Fellini film you saw and didn't understand. She's usually too sophisticted for sex.

7) **The Tease.** Remember, restraint is the key. Don't get your hopes up, or you're sure to be disappointed. Instead try for an intellectual experience and discuss Wimbledon, or Iraq's need for nuclear power.

8) **The Space Cadet.** Not just from Marin County, California. If you ask her where she's from, you're liable to hear something like, "Wherever you think I should be from." This kind of conversation is a dead giveaway. While astrological signs are a bit passe for today's cadet, cosmic revelations are standard. Ask yourself: *Is sexual gratification worth schizophrenia?*

THE SETTING

Unless you are a Successful Scammer (see preceding pages), the only real setting for the pickup is the party. These exist in various forms.

1) *The dorm party.* Not recommended, unless you happen to live in an extremely large dormitory containing several hundred people. Small dorms are simply too restrictive, and the odds of finding a compelling variety of the aforementioned types of College Woman are slim. Remember, you're not the only sexually-frustrated male present.

One more disadvantage to the dorm party pick-up: *reputation.* Gossip was invented in a freshman dorm, so think ahead if you live there. More than one freshman's sex life was extinguished the night he got drunk and tried to jump the R.A. who taught self-defense.

2) *The Frat Party.* The ideal mix of the various classifications of pick-up object. Depending on the college and the fraternity, the pick-up atmosphere can range from "perfect" to "real close." If you get her to your room, you've got it made; if not, move on to the next prospect. If you arrive after 11pm, employ the Direct Approach. This way, you either score fast or lose fast without further waste of time, effort and bad beer. Save those deep discussions on religion for the spontaneous, late-night, freshman rapping sessions. The frat party pick-up usually requires only a 100-word vocabulary.

The disadvantages? The majority of fraternity parties have large male-to-female ratios, sometimes on the order of 20:1. This requires clever strategy. The instant a girl is not dancing, talking, or making out with another guy- move in! Action is the key word here. Use speed above all else. For slower types, lumber over to the women's bathroom and catch them on their way out. Note: If all of the linemen from the football team show up for the party, this strategy becomes useless. Exercise caution.

WHERE TO TAKE HER

If she is a freshman, avoid her place. In the true spirit of dorm education, her roommate is probably a naive Mormon from Idaho. Instead, go to your room and lay it on the line with your roommate. Encourage him to learn to obey the tie-on-the-doorknob signal code. If he doesn't go for it, threaten to commit suicide because of a dismal social life. Remember, of course, that this is a two-way street. A Successful Scamming roommate could mean many nights on the dorm couch for you. If you have a single room, it's the ideal place, unless a night outdoors under the stars sounds more appealing. Leave the back seat of the car to Bob Seger and Bruce Springsteen; this is college! If you have a friend in the fraternity where a party is going on, use his room. But be sure to lock the door and take his key, or you're likely to find him stumbling in and climbing on both of you. Such menage-a-trois are pleasant only in Penthouse.

Don't be misled into thinking that college is one big pick-up scene. While that aspect is certainly present, many other students never come into contact with that sub-culture.

Some of these students are simply turned off by such techniques, and would rather meet a potential partner in another situation. Others subscribe to a different lifestyle: celibacy.

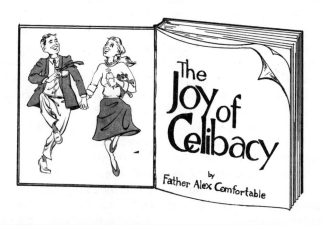

The Joy of Celibacy

by Father Alex Comfortable

Night Out

Sometimes you just have to get away from the academic and social constraints of the university. If you live nearby, you can always go home and watch TV. If not, you'll have to be a little more creative. Go out somewhere with a friend. This can be really fun if you live near a major city. Almost anything qualifies for the coveted day away, though you should be sure to match your destination to your mood, pocketbook, and partner's appearance.

Symphony. The best part about the symphony is that you get to dress up and be collegiate at the same time. Throw on your best suit and your old Nikes, grab a date, and head out for an evening amongst the city's elite.

Art Museum. Gives you a great excuse to put your hands behind your back while you're walking. As you look at the paintings, say things like "Well intended, but he doesn't quite achieve Hopper's sense of alie-

nation," or "I love wrought-iron sculpture." Make sure your date knows less about art than you.

Classy Bar. Assuming you're not underage (if you are, see fake ID section), this can be a great way to get to know someone, get drunk, and watch other people get to know people and get drunk. Though the drinks may be expensive, the atmosphere makes them almost worth it. It beats the campus pub, anyway.

Picnic In Park. As you sit beneath a maple, nibble Gouda, sip Chenin Blanc, discuss Diderot, and ignore the mosquitoes and ants. If you stay long enough, Hallmark Cards may come by and take a picture of you.

Dive Bar. Sleazy, but at least it's off campus. Your reflexes should be good enough to dodge beer bottles whizzing by your head, or at least to avoid the drunk at the bar who wants to tell you how important a college education is. Caution: Do NOT dress like a preppy.

Bowling Get back to school. Quick! (Take the shoes off first.)

Cinemascope

You'll probably enjoy going to the Flicks. Many students do. Gradually you'll realize that there are some films you've seen countless times, the films everybody has seen. Only Communists haven't seen The Wizard of Oz. These films are part of the curriculum; they are American culture.

Match the titles below with their proper plot synopses. A few fictitious films have been added to create a challenge.

A) The Rocky Horror Picture Show
B) The Wizard of Oz
C) The Graduate
D) Gone with the Transcript
E) Hannibal House

1) Faced with the choice between a promising career and an excellent graduate education, the homecoming track star chooses unabashed sex every night and thus becomes an instant hero in the college world. He drives an Alfa Romeo and wears dark sunglasses even at night, so who cares that he coughs spastically on his first cigarette?

2) The story of the very famous List of Courses and its devastating effect on the man who sought to use its force to gain entrance to grad school. See the fierce determination, the endless fury and the dashed hopes when North clashes against South, C- joins Incomplete, and F spoils all. Never before has so much been lost by so little. Never before has the role of antagonist been so effectively fulfilled by a slip of paper.

3) A couple spends a night in the haunted house of a mad scientist sporting the latest in women's lingerie.

4) Who delivered 100,000 Carthaginians to the Roman barbeque? Who mixed arsenic with the sacrificial wine? Who stampeded Commencement with 89 elephants? Every Ides of March the trees are filled with computer paper, every Senate meeting the toilets explode, but the wackiness doesn't stop there. The good fun twists and shouts till morn as the partiers loot and sack their own house! Road trips over the Alps and devastating routs top off the wild antics during this college-crazed extravaganza.

5) SAT scores and cap'n'gown worries are brushed aside by a nineteen-year-old swashbuckler

as she makes her way down the golden path of fortune. Befriending munchkin and lion alike, she wastes the local witch and lowers inflation, thus attaining instant popularity. Yet just as the crowd becomes ecstatic, she hangs up her career and goes home. She later goes on to law school.

Ten
Rules
Of
Tanning

Though you may not be a Bo Derek or George Hamilton when it comes to tanning, you should at least give it your best shot, especially since you're in college and you have some extra time on your hands. True, it can be difficult in a place like Vermont, but with the proper guidance (and a modicum of sunshine) even the palest can become a tanning god or goddess.

1) **Learn the vocabulary.** Don't "tan." Instead, "Bag some rays" or "catch some UV's (ultraviolet rays)." Get off on the right foot by letting people know you're a serious tanner.

2) **Have the right equipment.** Small tanning chair, designer sunglasses (see Clothes Minded), Hawaiian tanning lotion, obnoxious clothing (Men: loud shorts; Women: two-tone Dolfin shorts and flashy bathing suit).

3) **Hair.** Guys: short hair. Girls: any length as long as it doesn't block the sun. Should be blonde if possible. Don't hesitate to apply a little lemon juice if necessary.

4) **Blare beach music** from your box to let everyone know you're bagging rays. Getting up to change the tape is a great way to keep from studying.

5) **Keep a frisbee** close by to throw to passing friends. Say things like, "Off to the library? Give me my frisbee back."

6) **Don't be the first** to rush out and catch UV's on the first sunny day of the year. This is an obvious indication that the sun never shines in your home-town. Let the people from Antarctica and Maine go ahead of you.

7) **Tan each side** of your body evenly. And remember not to fall asleep with your hand on your stomach, as this can make for embarassing comments.

8) **There's no such thing** as a free lunch. Remember, if you want to be tan, you've got to get out there and work at it, every possible moment. Study at night, tan during the day.

9) **Go to the beach** at least once a year, no matter how far away you live. Just as devout Catholics should get to Rome once a year, so should any sun tanner make it to the beach. There you can learn from the pros.

10) **Never admit** that you have been burned (*fried*, in tanning jargon). A fried body can ruin the reputation of any tanning god or goddess.

A Change of Pace

College is in part an effort to test your limits by removing old social norms and redefining your set of guidelines by which to live. College is a time to learn and a time to experiment. So get crazy. You only go around once. If you need some help finding original and crazy ideas, there are a few standards that can't go wrong.

1) **Attend a formal dance wearing informal clothes.** Show up in a swimming suit at an elegant tea dance. Not only will the old people go crazy, but if you're obscene enough you'll get in the paper.

2) **Attend a final in formal garb.** Almost the opposite of attending a formal dance wearing informal clothes. Show up at a final with tux or gown and champagne. If the final turns out to be too tough, you can always drink the bubbly.

3) **Run for head of Student Government on Free Sex slate.** *Caution:* if you win and don't deliver your campaign promises, your popularity will nose dive.

Dine And Dash

Probably the most famous food scam, and the one most people are familiar with, is the Dine and Dash method. A favorite with college students and skid row bums, this plan involves going to a restaurant, ordering and eating a full meal, and leaving immediately without paying the bill.

If you plan to Dine and Dash (and if you're on the Scammer's Meal Plan, it's a must) remember some of these tips.

1. Sit at a table close to an exit.
2. Plan your escape route; have a getaway car, or at worst, a clear path for running.
3. Always make sure the meal costs more than what you'd ordinarily pay.
4. Don't forget to order dessert.

Note: If you get caught, try to talk the management into letting you wash dishes. You can't "serve and dash" the city jail.

Special Note: If you dine and dash at an Italian restaurant, be prepared never to see your family again.

SIX

LUST
TO
LOVE

RELATION-
SHIPS

Two important aspects of college life are dating and relationships, and here too you must learn to make the adjustment from high school to college. While there will always be a few college students - homecoming queens, Rose Bowl MVP's, models who can continue to date in college using the same techniques they used in high school, most kids will find drastic changes in the "dating game" when they get to college.

Unless you go to college with all of your closest friends, chances are you will arrive on campus without much of a social reputation, and unless you're a leper or the most independent person who has ever lived, you'll want to do something about this. Assuming that you are relatively normal, you'll probably want to go out on a date sooner or later.

"So what's the big deal?" you might ask. "College dating can't be that much different, can it?" First of all, you must realize that your reign as king or queen of the hill is over after high school and so are the days of lying by the pool waiting for dates to call (because you were the hit of the high school play).

Group Dating

Many people at college discover that their first dates tend to be what are referred to "group dates." The ideal group date usually consists of 10-15 people who go on an excursion to a local venue (Chinese restaurants are always good) or a college-sponsored event (the campus movie is popular), spend little money, and have a good time. The group date is popular for a number of reasons:

1) **Economics.** Since you won't have to "pick up the tab" for anyone else and since you will usually be going to an inexpensive place, group dates are generally thrifty outings.

2) **Friendship.** You can get to know a large group of people pretty well without having to go through the motions of superficiality and trying to impress anyone.

3) **Security.** Most of the activity that takes place on a group date is playful and harmless, and most of the relationships are platonic, so you'll be able to show a little affection without applying any one-on-one pressure.

All things considered, the group date is a good introduction to college dating, and provides you with the chance to meet people, thus leading up to "individual dates."

Dates For The Non-Dater

Asking someone out on a big date can be tough. It's expensive, time-consuming, and may prove to be worthless if the person doesn't like you. Luckily, the low pressure environment of college affords a solution. You can spend time with someone without officially dating.

Studying with someone. *"What did you get for number two?"* means *"I love you"* to the experienced non-dater.

Going to the campus movie. Usually a good, though not first-run film and the admission (you each pay for your own ticket) is only a dollar or two. No one could call this a date.

Going to the campus pub or coffee house. A conversation over a glass of beer or a cup of coffee. Can be seen as nothing more than a study break.

Eating dinner at the cafeteria. How could anyone ever expect love to bloom over a plate of creamed fish? The non-dater knows that it happens all the time.

Visiting someone's room. Very innocuous and very good. Just pretend your borrowing some albums.

Individual Dating

By now you're sick of eating Chinese food every Friday with 20 other people. It's time for an individual date: one-on-one, just like the old days. As mentioned earlier, you won't get any dates simply by strolling across campus in your Kelso High letterman's jacket; individual dates in college occur in a much different manner.

An old favorite among many college students is the "On-Campus Date." This involves going with your date to a spot on campus; it's an accessible, entertaining, and usually an inexpensive way to get to know someone better. It usually works best when you are first going out with somebody because it doesn't seem too serious and, if the date turns out to be a dud, you haven't wasted any gas driving to some fancy spot 15 miles from campus.

Once you've grown tired of the on-campus spots, or if you are really trying to impress someone, you will most likely want to take him or her on an "off campus date." Naturally, off-campus dates take place off campus, and can be anything from a candlelit dinner at an expensive restaurant to a Blondie concert in a small club. Escaping the campus atmosphere can do wonders for a date, since it is a good chance to get to know your partner in a non-academic situation, as well as remind you that, yes, there is life past Bio 40.

One final thing which must be mentioned is the so-called "unique date." Definitely a college phenomenon, the unique date occurs when someone tries to impress someone else by taking them on a non-conforming date. College students love to get dressed up in formal garb, pick up their dates in a chauffered limosine, and then go eat at McDonald's or go out for a beer in the sleaziest bar in the city just for the hell of it. You probably should indulge in at least one unique date during your undergraduate years, because when you become branch manager of the Indiana Federal Bank, you won't be able to engage in anything out of the ordinary, for fear that the public will think you're a college student.

How to Impress Chicks

Impressive	Not Impressive
BMW	Old Buick (in the shop)
Single room	Top bunk bed
Carte Blanche card	Fenstown Library card (out of date)
Steel string guitar in corner	Kazoo on desk

Halston blazer	High school letterman's jacket
Expensive brunch at Hyatt	Breakfast squares on bus
Being quarterback of the football team	Being manager of the bowling team
"Has anyone ever told you you look like Meryl Streep?"	*"Is that a birthmark on your face?"*
"Are you sure you want to walk all the way home in the cold?"	*"Wanna sack out here?"*

How to Impress Guys

Impressive	*Not Impressive*
Apartment with own room	Two curious roommates
Picasso print on wall	Stains on wall
Beef Wellington, caviar, and wine	Hot dogs, baked beans, and Dr. Pepper
Capricious jump in fountain	Accidental fall in sewer

Black-tie formal at Congressman's house	Beer and pretzels at County Coroner's office
Whispering in his ear	Throwing up in his sink
"My dad's friends think he has a shot at becoming Senator."	*"My dad's friends think he has a shot at getting paroled."*
"Hey, want to play some backgammon?"	*"Hey, want to help me do the dishes?"*
"What was your phone number again?"	*"What was your name again?"*

Dating Famous

People's Kids

Many schools get their share of students whose parents are prominent and even though these kids have been raised in an incredibly different atmosphere than you, they are still students. Despite their upbringing and family position, you can treat these people as you would anyone else. Notice them. Make eyes at them in the library. Lust after them. Ask them out. Take them out. Go steady with them. Cheat on them. Drop them for someone else.

You must remember one thing: *DO NOT BE INTIMI-DATED*. So what if her dad is Menachem Begin's best friend, and who cares if his mom owns half of Canada? These kids are still young, free-spirited college students like yourself, and are almost always up for a good time. So, get your confidence up, act naturally, and who knows, maybe someday you'll make the cover of People magazine.

Advantages

1) They're often extremely wealthy.

2) You can impress your friends at home ("Hey Bucky, guess what? I'm dating Mao's daughter").

3) If you actually have a lasting relationship, you'll probably be set for life with a good job - or at the least some connections.

4) Personal satisfaction: when you see your boyfriend's dad on television, you can smile to yourself because you know what his kid looks like without clothes on.

5) You can discover interesting secrets about your partner's parents and write a revealing and lucrative expose for the National Enquirer.

Disadvantages

1) Sometimes you end up sacrificing looks and personality.

2) More often than not these kids have some psychological problems.

3) Since they're used to "life in the fast lane," dates and presents will deplete your savings account in about two weeks.

4) Someday you will meet his or her parents, and you'll never measure up to their standards.

5) They're often Republicans, homosexuals, or Yankee fans.

A Story of Intermajor Dating

I really didn't know what I was getting into. Here I was, a History major, and she, a Computer Science major. I needed help typing a paper into a computer, and there she was.

They told me it would never work. I spoke English and she spoke Fortran. Hell, this was Georgia in 1967; people of different majors didn't even talk to each other, let alone go out together.

Still, we tried. I thought my parents would kill me when they met her. "Jim Bob?" My father cornered me in the kitchen. "What'd I tell ya 'bout datin' non-History majors, boy? If you wanna have a chance at inheritin' Grandpa's encyclopedias, you'd better wise up."

I was young then, and I didn't believe him. Her beautiful hands as they punched the keys meant more to me in those days than life else. We eloped, yet my father's words echoed ceaselessly in my mind: "Boy, she'll do ya wrong."

Then the tension began. The arguments, the fights, the calculators whizzing past my ear at dinner. The relationship began to show the strain. "Your problem is you're not human!" I screamed. "That does not compute" was her cold reply.

It was soon thereafter that we split, she heading for the Silicon Valley of California and I for the ivied walls of academia in the Northeast. I think about her now and then, and I still recall my father's warning: "Intermajor dating is trouble, boy."

The Hometown Honey's Visit

The visit from the Hometown Honey (HTH) is as much a part of college as graduation. For most, the visit is a joyful reunion and a chance to patch up any strain that going to different colleges may have put on the relationship. It can also be an opportunity to impress your friends. This romantic rendez-vous may do wonders for you in the eyes of your peers, who until now might have thought that you were a bit of a loser. Dinners, shows, trips around campus, and for the first time a chance to be really alone with your lover can give the HTH visit all of the ingredients of a romantic movie.

1) *The Arrival: a long-awaited embrace.*

2) *Playing tennis.*

3) *A Table for Two.*

4) *The Good-bye: a soft tear.*

On the other hand, not all HTH visits are stories out of Victorian novels. Some appear more like chapters out of a sleazy magazine from a Cleveland dime store. If you've already started a new relationship and you'd rather forget the old one, or if you've been starting a new relationship with a different person every night, then you'd probably rather your former paramour didn't show.

1) *The Arrival: a long-awaited hitch.*

2) *Playing Pac-man.*

3) *A Table for Trash.*

4) *The Good-bye: a soft squeeze.*

Different Ways to Say You're a Virgin

There is a wide variation of sexual experience within the average college environment so you shouldn't feel inferior or somehow less worthy if you haven't had as much experience as others. On the other hand, if you are a virgin you will need an effective, acceptable way to say that your sexual record remains pristine. Try one of these college standards the next time someone asks you, *"Are you a virgin?"*

"Yes."

"Not really. But I haven't had sex yet."

"You bet. Pass the sugar."

"I can't answer that question. It's too personal."

"Well, once I . . .I could have . . . I . . . I don't know . . . I've seen a lot of movies."

"Who, me? No way! This chastity belt is just for show."

"Me? Are you kidding? No way! I go out all the time!

Every week I date someone new. Sex is one thing I don't have to worry about."

"Sex is a sacred thing. It's not something to be taken lightly. If I had wanted, I could have had sex lots of times, but I feel that it's the ultimate display of affection to another person, and I want to save myself for the person I marry."

"I've got a lot of things going right now and I just don't have the time for sex."

"If you mean have I had sex, no."

Spot the Virgin

There are always a few of them and they are always the topic of extreme wonderment or alienation. They are usually cute, always nice, and some of them date tremendous numbers of people. They have a tendency to get their assignments in on time and belong to dozens of campus groups. Some attend church regularly and never talk about sex. Others never go to church and always talk about sex. They are always philosophical and seem to believe that one can actually learn important things while at college.

Though they try their best to fit into the mainstream, something still gives them away. See if you can spot the virgin.

A Conversation

Sometimes students tend to keep new affairs hushed because they want to appear modest, but if you can get them to disclose a little, the rest will follow.

Elvira: Jenny, I was talking to Carrie the other day and she said that you have a new boyfriend.

Jenny: Yeah. You know Eric, don't you? I've been seeing him a lot lately.

Elvira: Really? So you two are pretty serious, huh?

Jenny: Well, we've been dating for a while now . . .

Elvira: Wow, so you two are going together?

Jenny: Well, it's more than that. We . . . we spend almost all of our time together.

Elvira: Oh, I see . . . the old "sneak back to the room before dawn" trick.

Jenny (blushing): Yes, well, we have spent the night together . . .

Elvira: Really? The whole night? You two are sleeping together?

Jenny: I . . . (stammers) . . . that is . . . we . . . fool around a little.

Elvira: Jenny! You're kidding!

Jenny: It's no big deal. We both love and respect each other, and I think that we're both mature enough to handle making love.

Elvira: Wow, that's great.

Jenny: Yeah. God, it's so great to be getting it on regularly . . .

Elvira: I'm envious.

Jenny: You should be. We're doing it constantly . . . and in every way imaginable. By the way, can I borrow a quart of Mazola?

A Little Flair

The bed can become a boring place to have sex if you've been "doing it" there for quite some time. It's not a very unusual place to "do it" and it's so traditional that the thought of cuddling between the sheets with your lover in the late evening doesn't show any imagination or sense of adventure. After all, isn't college supposed to be about adventure, excitement, spirit, and foolishness? Why not risk it one night and sack out on the golf course?

If you decide to take the plunge, and you're willing to try new places, but you still consider yourself a bit conservative, here's some advice. Start out slowly, and try a 'novice adventurer.'

For the Novice Adventurer

1) **Roommate's bed.** This is like doing it in your parents' bed.

2) **Top of pool table.** Definitely classy (Burt Reynolds and Dyan Cannon did it in *Shamus*).

3) **Water bed filled with goldfish.** Keep the cat away.

Around Campus (more daring)

1) **Stopped library elevator (between floors).** Expect a smirk from the librarian when the doors open.

2) **Under the computer terminals.** While the computer nerds are up above contemplating Pascal, you two can be logged in down below.

3) **Back row of large lecture hall** while watching boring documentary. More interesting than the film . . . especially for the other students in the class.

Around Town (most daring)

1) **During long flight,** when the lights are out. Kind of like in the movies. You've always dreamed of doing this one!

2) **In school fountain.** If anyone sees you, fake a statue pose.

3) **During an interview.** You might not get the job.

Dating by Phone

Asking a girl out is never easy, especially on the phone.

1) **Decide which girl to ask out.** Look up name and number in student phone directory.

2) **Number not there.** Have second thoughts about asking someone out. She's probably seen The J. Geils Band twice before.

3) **Discover number** on course syllabus in wallet.

4) **Dial first four numbers,** hesitate, then hang up.

5) **Have second thoughts.** She most likely has a boyfriend.

6) **Friend passes by room.** He mentions that your prospective date wishes she had boyfriend to take her to J. Geils concert.

7) **Hope renewed.** Pick up phone and dial number.

8) **Busy.** She's probably being asked to J. Geils concert. Hang up.

9) **Get depressed.** Put on J. Geils album. Blow off whole thing.

10) **Phone rings.** It's her. She has two front row seats to J. Geils and wants you to go. Say yes. Hang up. Jump for joy.

Photo courtesy Stanford University

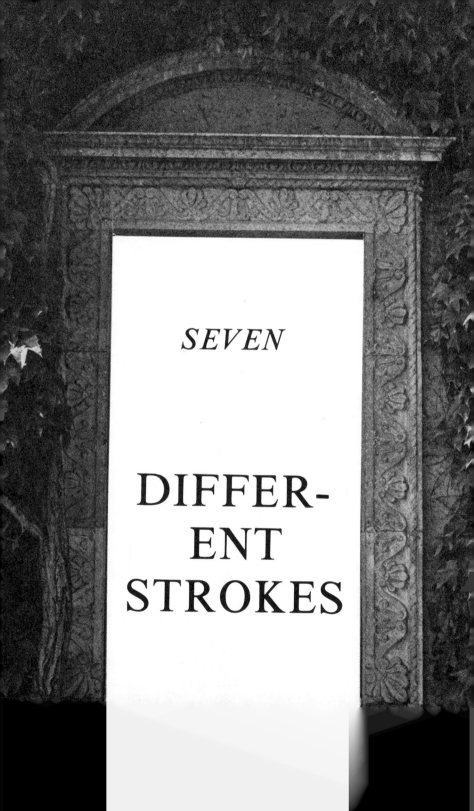

SEVEN

DIFFER-
ENT
STROKES

COLLEGE MEETS THE REAL WORLD

After nine months of Sartre, Newton, and Keynes, you're ready for a break. That's why God created summer. Summer is a chance to get away from the academic and social grind of college. It's also a chance to kick back and relax.

If you're like most students, you'll probably spend the summer at home with your family. The pace will be much slower there than at college and you'll be expected to get a job and spend some time around the house. For the most part, your summer will be reserved for two things: making money and blowing it. That's your God-given right, and that's what makes the summer so great.

You may have a summer fling, where you meet someone at the office, at a bar, or at a pool and proceed to have a full-fledged relationship. Or you may be catching up on (or patching up on) a longdistance relationship. Either way, summer always goes by too fast.

By the end of the summer, you can't believe there ever was a time during the first week when you were bored to death. You always end up having a good time so that when the end of the summer comes and the tarps start going over the swimming pools and the luggage starts getting packed, you may entertain a momentary tinge of sadness at having to go back to school. But it will pass, and before you know it, you'll be right back into the swing of college.

Incredible Summers

The great thing about being in college is that you're allowed to be a little crazy. In fact, you're encouraged to be a little crazy. So why go home in the summer and work in an office or factory when you can do something wild and fun? You should line up something spectacular for the summer so you'll really shine in the eyes of your friends when you get back to school in the fall.

1) **Work overseas.** *Ou est la Plage Publique? Viva il Papa!* This can be a great experience. You can do a wide variety of jobs ranging from picking grapes to giving guided tours. Meet the natives, learn the language, catch the diseases. Drawback: it's hard to find *All in the Family* reruns.

2) **Set a record** for the *Guinness Book of World Records.* The record for singing Frank Sinatra's greatest hits while in-haling goldfish and building a condominium is only 67 days. If you started right when you got home, you could easily sur-pass it. Drawback: many people lapse into a coma after singing "New York, New York" more than a dozen times.

3) **Play major league baseball.** You get to travel all over the United States, you stay in shape, and you have the chance to be on nationwide TV. The money's great, and it looks good on your resume. Besides, it's the nation-al pastime. Drawbacks: you have to be pretty good and you won't get to play in the World Series since it starts in October and classes usually begin in Sep-tember.

4) **Climb Mount Everest.** Ed-mund Hilary did it and got knighted. How about you? Plen-ty of fresh air and exercise, and the view is great. Drawbacks: if you fall you might get hurt.

A Novel Plan

Summer means going home to mindless days in the sun and mindless nights in front of the TV. Somehow you have to combat the entropy that's sure to set in. How? Books. If college has taught you anything, it's that reading expands your mind and improves you as a person. You can't let yourself slip.

In reality, however, it's probably a little harder than you think to read great works while you're working at Chuck's Bakery or climbing Mount Everest. In fact, *Lady Chatterly's Lover* doesn't rate with *Leave it to Beaver* reruns. The real world is designed to make you an intellectual maladroit and no matter how hard you try, you will eventually succumb.

These truths become evident when you contemplate the books you'll plan to read and the ones you'll actually read.

Planned Reading	**Actual Reading**
1) *Le Petit Prince*	*The Royal Baby*
2) *All the King's Men*	*All the President's Men*
3) *The Bible*	*The World According to Garp*
4) *Much Ado about Nothing*	*The Official Preppy Handbook*
5) *Animal Farm*	*Garfield Goes on a Diet*
6) *Grapes of Wrath*	*Winemaking in the Home*
7) *The Old Man and the Sea*	*Yachting the Great Lakes*
8) *Fahrenheit 451*	*Body Heat*
9) *Jane Eyre*	*Jane Fonda's Workout Book*
10) *Les Miserables*	*A Few Minutes with Andy Rooney*
11) *Oedipus Rex*	*The Joy of Sex*

The 90-day Career

You'll probably be expected to work during the summer, unless you're in line for an oil fortune or you're in an iron lung. Never mind that the job might be mopping up water at Death Valley for $2.10 an hour; parents like to see their kids working. Industriousness is still held to be a virtue and you're expected to embrace it. They're trying to make you a good citizen and a good citizen works. Period.

Besides, what would you do if you didn't work? Things can get pretty dull around town even when you're working. The money you'll make will come in handy for those new speakers you need. Jobs are good for resumes. You make business contacts and gain valuable working experience by entering the job world during the summer. Enough of this; we're beginning to sound like the Career Center.

Once you've decided that you're going to work during the summer, the next step is finding a job. Start looking early. You've got to remember that there are millions of other college students like you out there looking for the same jobs. Write everyone you know who might be able to help. Talk to people. Ask around. Use any available contact. Date the mayor's daughter. Marry the governor's son. If you know the right methods and contacts, getting the job of your choice should be no problem.

Taking Liberties

Once you're hired, make the job your own. Start slowly, by coming in at 8:15 instead of at 8 o'clock. Then start typing letters on company stationery and company time. With these trivialities behind you, you can begin to assert yourself. Have your friends drop by to chat. Take a day off to go camping with your friends. Call overseas friends on the company phone. Sit in the boss's chair and tell the secretary to come in and take dictation. Order the company's stocks liquidated. Order the company ledgers altered, then call the IRS to report that you have discovered a tax fraud. Have the building destroyed.

In the
Christmas Spirit

The first Christmas means more than just another chance to go home (or the first chance if you didn't go home for Thanksgiving). For many, it has the added attraction of being the end of the quarter or semester. That means that when you turn in the last exam book and walk back to your room, you're done. Finished. No more work. All that's left is packing and bumming a ride to the airport to fly home, or hopping in the car and driving home. Even if your exams are after Christmas, you can't beat that feeling of exhilaration of knowing that you can take it easy with family and friends for the next month or so.

Christmas takes on a new significance once you've been to college. No longer is it a time for eating, getting blasted, and opening presents. Now it is a time for family reunions, eating, getting blasted, and opening presents.

Your relatives will all ask, "So, how's college, Johnny?" To this, you have to be firm and

reply, "Fine. John . . . call me John." Though your parents will be proud of the new independence you have gained at college, you'll be amazed at how fast they treat you like the same old kid. You'll be taking out the trash and doing the dishes in no time.

Christmas is a great time to see old friends. You can trade stories about school and even brag, subtly, that your school is better. When your friend tells you that her college was #8 in football, you can reply, "Gee, that's great! Most of the guys on your team weren't admitted to my school. That stupid admissions officer!"

The parties will be the same as high school parties except for some notable differences. The high school slob will have gone preppy. The high school teetotaler will slam ten brews. The high school klutz will be a dancing king, and the high school beauty will be dressed in jeans and a flannel shirt and smoking a joint.

You'll come home from the

party and answer your parents' questions about your friends. "Oh, she's fine." "He's great, making straight A's." "She must have put on 20 pounds." You'll be saying to yourself, "I hope they don't realize that I am completely smashed." Then you'll saunter off to bed while your parents watch *The Tonight Show*.

Aside from seeing old friends, you'll devote some of your Christmas time to doing the traditionals: baking cakes and cookies with the brothers and sisters, putting up the tree and decorations, and watching a lot of TV specials. You may have planned to do some reading but forget it; you'll have enough of

that to do when you get back. For now you should just take it easy.

As far as presents go, don't worry. It's not uncommon for a college student to go Christmas shopping at the campus bookstore. "Oh, boy, a college sweatshirt!" yells little brother. "Hey, a college sweater!" says sister. "A college shot glass," beams Dad. "Oh, how thoughtful! A college toilet seat," notes Mom. Presents from the bookstore are sure-fire winners; the brothers and sisters can wear them to their school and impress their friends and Mom and Dad can think of you every time they use the bathroom.

The Christmas vacation is topped off with a complete New Year's bash where everyone gets together and gets drunk to loud music and insipid conversation. Sometimes, however, the big New Year's Party doesn't quite come together and you end up watching "New Year's Rockin' Eve With Dick Clark at Times Square."

The new year marks the beginning of the denouement. From here on in, you'll be saying your last goodbyes and preparing for the next semester. This is usually a time of mixed feelings: excitement to be going back to new friends but sadness to be leaving old ones. Soon you'll be back at school and the Christmas break will be little more than a fond smile and special photographs.

Christmas Specials
For
College Students

1. *Rudolph the Red-Nosed Reindeer.*
2. *How the Grinch Stole Christmas.*
3. *Frosty the Snowman.*
4. *Christmas With the King Family.*
5. *Santa Claus Is Comimg To Town.*
6. *Christmas In Afghanistan.*
7. *Santa Claus Flunks Organic Chemistry.*
8. *Frosty the Coke Dealer.*

Living In The Real World

It can be a little frustrating when college meets the real world. If your college is in a sleepy town, chances are that the town has been sleeping for years and nothing you or your friends can do will wake it up.

The fast pace of college may at one time or another become too fast for you. Tests, studies, parties, relationships, and day to day living take up all of your time. It's easy to forget that there's a real world out there. Russia could invade Detroit and you'd never know.

Time Out

Most schools permit students to take off time and get away from the college scene if they choose to do so during their four year bout with academic grind, social pressures, and indecision concerning post-graduate life. At some schools, this is called "stopping out." For many students, summer suffices in providing an alternative to college and in allowing students to let off steam. For many others, summer is just not enough.

Reasons for stopping out commonly fall into two categories. Either the student seeks escape and relaxation, or he or she seeks free time to pursue an activity which demands more time than a full-time student can give. The first is often called "bumming out," not to be confused with "being bummed out." If you decide to stop out (or bum out) you'll want to do something really special (or really low key).

Ambitious Stop Outs

Effect nuclear arms reductions among world powers.
Run for Congress.
Teach hieroglyphics at rival college.
Merge two large oil corporations.
Start your own university.

Bumming Out versus Stopping Out

Things To Do:	Things To Do:
Nothing.	Everything.
Go home and watch reruns of *The Price is Right*.	Produce own T.V. show.
Watch grass grow.	Watch real estate empire grow.
Become a regular at a local bar.	Become a regular on *Meet the Press*.
Hitchhike across Europe.	Invade Europe.

Real World Intrusions

College has never been confused with the so-called "real world." In fact, once you get to school, you'll probably forget that there is such a thing as a 9 to 5 job, since your schedule is pretty flexible, except for classes and meals.

To prevent you from sinking completely into a "college mentality," there are some people around campus who will serve as reminders that there is more to life than midterms and come-as-your-roommate parties. These folks work 9 to 5 like the rest of the "real world," and as a result, they cannot accept or relate to the fact that you are a carefree, careless college student with a loose schedule and no conception of the working world. As a student, watch out for these "real world intrusions"; you'll find them at every school.

1) **Office Workers.** These people actually can relate, but they don't want to. Chances are they graduated from your school, but they're locked into a 9 to 5 job in which the most exciting moment occurs when the water cooler breaks. They're often rude and officious, and their schedules never coincide with yours. Last day to pay that $1000 tuition? The only free time you have is at noon between Geology class and Chemistry lab? Sorry . . .it's lunch time in the real world.

2) **Maintenance Workers.** A total dose of reality. These people barely know the name of your college; to them, it's just the company that keeps the Pop Tarts on the table and the Bud in the fridge. They have no concept of classes, and that lawn has to be mowed, so just as the professor gets to the key point about Faulkner's treatment of women, count on the roar of a 450 horsepower engine drowning out any words of wisdom.

3) **Cooks.** These people are a breed apart. Anyone who cooks for obnoxious, spoiled college

kids has got to be a different sort. The best thing about cooks is that they make you stop and think about how uncomplicated college life really is; it's easy when you realize that these people are paying their rent by feeding you lasagna.

4) **Construction Workers.** You need to sleep in until nine o'clock for a change because it's been a rough week. You can count on some great shuteye, right? Wrong. The sewer pipe outside has to be dug up, and the men from Off-Campus Construction are there at eight cranking up the heavy equipment and yelling to each other at the top of their lungs. On lunch break these guys set the Feminist movement back 55 years with their obnoxious comments.

5) **Visitors.** Easy to spot, since they're too old to be students and not dressed eclectically enough to be professors. These people inevitably show up only when you're on a tight schedule. For visitors, it's almost a necessity to get lost on a college campus, so as you hurry to your history final, be prepared to be stopped and asked,"Do you know where our daughter's dorm is? It's called *Something Hall.*"

Collegiate Syndromes

Once you settle comfortably into the collegiate environment, you'll begin to develop what is commonly referred to as the "college mentality." Everything revolves around college; you begin to develop your own vocabulary, your own sense of fun, and even your own culture. One important result of this is that you begin to evolve into a total college student, and since the school itself acts as a giant, self-containing bubble, you never stand out as a student until you venture into the real world. The following list explains some of the ways in which one can identify or be identified as a college student. They'll seem like nothing at all to you, but be forewarned: they're obvious signs to anyone not in the college community.

1) **The Movie Theatre Response Syndrome.** What hath the *Rocky Horror Picture Show* wrought? Going to a movie on a college campus is like going to a combination night club/-survival course. If you're not being verbally assaulted by the back row comedians, you're being literally pelted with oranges or paper airplanes. Humorous responses to lines from the movie are an accepted part of campus etiquette, but once you get out into the real world, look out. The 6'4" lumberjack behind you wants to hear Burt Reynolds, not a collegiate wisecracker.

2) **The Omnipresent Beer Syndrome.** When you were younger, remember how you used to make fun of those "losers" who had a can of beer with them wherever they went? Well guess what? In college this takes on a new dimension. First, you'll realize how great it is to be able to have beer in your dorm. Then you'll start taking it to football games, movies, and even lectures. The next logical step is carting your brew off campus, and when you stroll into the A&P or First Interstate Bank with a Lowenbrau in tow, be prepared for a shock: it really is illegal, so the police

may be called in. Off-campus cops don't mess around, either.

3) **The Loudness/Irreverance Syndrome.** At college you can say pretty much anything, to anyone, and at any volume. Irreverance is all part of the game (don't try to say it's not fun to call Einstein an "idiot" or Martin Luther a "wildman") when you're a college student with no worries. When you take it off campus, however, "irreverance" often becomes translated into "obnoxiousness": opera patrons probably won't consider a BA from the balcony in the same light as would your dormmates, and a food fight in Elaine's won't elicit the response that it would in the campus cafeteria.

Five Preppy Ways To Say Beer, Brews, Brewskis, Roadies, Beevos.

1. Beer
2. Brews
3. Brewskis
4. Roadies
5. Beevos

The Big Change

Transferring can be a confusing issue for those who are confused. Transferring can be a frightening issue for those who are frightened. Transferring can be a small issue for those who are small. But no matter how much is written on the subject, a few commonly asked questions persist.

There are basically two types of transfers: one who plans to transfer all along, or the other who realizes he made a mistake in selecting colleges. The first type will probably be wearing a class ring of another school. The second may be found off in a corner somewhere mumbling to itself, "What am I doing here?" If you find yourself doing either of these, read on.

Q. Would transferring be right for me?
A. Well, that depends on who you are. First you must ask yourself, "who am I?"

Q. Who am I?
A. That depends on where you're from, what course you've pursued, and what time you hit the sack at night. Transferring ultimately comes down to whether you like where you are now.

Q. Do I like where I am now?
A. How's the food?

Q. How do I know what other schools are like?
A. Don't bother reading the school bulletins. As you've discovered at your own school, the beautiful chick and that incredibly cute guy who appear every other page in the bulletin are nowhere to be found at the school itself. Visit schools instead.

Q. How will I know which schools to visit?
A. Where are your friends from high school going? Surely you don't think everyone in your entire senior class made a huge mistake!

Q. How can I tell, by visiting, if a school is any better?
A. Look for obvious signs of abounding good times: an overall sense of euphoria shared by the student body, dancing girls, and flashing neon lights.

Q. *What if I apply and don't get in?*
A. This probably means you were rejected. Go into your room, lean against the window sill, and sing, "Where is love?"

Q. *Will I fit in as a transfer?*
A. Yes, but you'll have to learn to disregard such remarks as "Oh, so you couldn't get in the first time, right?" "Why did you transfer? You don't fit in at all!" or "slime!"

Q. *What is life as a transfer like?*
A. Pretty much the same. Eating, sleeping, and watching "General Hospital" continues.

Q. *How many students transfer each year?*
A. More than one. In fact, lots do. Tons.

Q. *Why do students transfer?*
A. Sometimes students transfer to content themselves. Other times it is to take advantage of another school's particular department superiority. Rarely do students transfer because of dirty shower curtains.

Q. *Should I transfer?*
A. Are you content? Is your present school satisfactory in the field of study you have chosen? Are the shower curtains clean?

Q. *Where else can I learn about transferring?*
A. Of course, there are many other books and resources to help you learn about tranferring, but you'll never really learn unless you transfer a few times.

FROM HERE TO THERE

From	To
An East Coast school	A West Coast school
A West Coast school	Another West Coast school
An inner city school	Anywhere
A school in the country	Anywhere (except an inner city school)
Your Dad's school	Your Mom's school
Your Mom's school	Your sister's school
Your sister's school	A friend's school
A friend's school	A job

Parent's Day

Having your parents visit you at school is a little like winning an all-expense paid trip to Akron; it probably won't be harmful, but what's the point of it? Once you become settled in the college environment, you begin to feel that it is your own domain, and any intrusion from the home front will be nothing but a restriction on your new independence.

The Five Worst Things About Your Parents Visiting

1) You'll have to miss a night or two of partying to go out to dinner with them.

2) You'll have to clean up your room.

3) You can't swear.

4) You and your girlfriend or boyfriend will have to go through the motions of actual "dating" lest your parents think there is anything more to the relationship.

5) You'll have to try to convince them that that bong on your desk is a dehumidifier.

The Five Best Things About Your Parents Visiting

1) They'll bring you money.
2) They'll bring you money.
3) They'll bring you money.
4) They'll bring you money.
5) They'll bring you money.

Take the Money And Run

The rich, especially the super-rich, have little trouble paying for college. And the poor are so deprived and underprivileged that they'll never get a chance at a college education unless they receive a lot of aid. That leaves the middle class.

Since the middle class has the most difficulty obtaining financial aid, many ways of making ends meet have evolved. These include everything from beating the system ("stealing a college education") to not going to college because it's too expensive.

The first step to benefitting from any financial aid is getting it, so start putting yourself in a class apart from the millions of other applicants, all of whom consider themselves worthy of aid.

There are many ways of "stretching" the truth. Owners of businesses can disguise their balance sheets for a particular year. Likewise, some financial whizzes are able to write off college expenses by making them appear as donations to charity.

Bad Examples Of Financial Aid Applications

1) **Family dog as dependent.** *Fido Peterson, age 7 -* that's 49 for you and me.

2) **Obvious cheating on income.** Occupation: *president, General Motors.* Income: *$7,000.00 per annum.*

3) **Blatant depreciation of assets.** Automobile: *1982 Mercedes 450SL.* Estimated worth: *$4000.00 wear and tear driving to the country club .*

4) **Large tax write-offs.** Investments: *$2,000,000.00 loss from selling war insur-* *ance in Iraq.*

5) **Questionable occupations.** Name: *Bruce Wayne.* Occupation: *Millionaire (and crime fighter).* Name: *Giuseppe Cannelloni.* Occupation: *Linen cleaning service.* Income: *$450,000.00*

6) **Begging.** *In order to pay for Kelly's college education, we would have to forego having the yacht painted next year. Could you please give use some financial aid?*

First Aid

Your financial aid will probably come in many forms, and this is generally called "the package." The package contains one or more of the following:

Loan. From Uncle Sam in the form of an NDSL, an approval to obtain a HELP loan from your local bank, a GSL, or a loan from the school itself. If you don't get a loan of some kind from your school, see your nearest bank, or talk to Chico at the corner of 5th and Main.

Grant. Free money. Like pennies from Heaven, grants don't ever have to be paid back. The bigger the grant, the happier Dad & Mom will be.

Job. You may be requested to find a job during the school year. They'll call this "self-help." Despite all the aid available, you'll still be able to tell your children how you "worked your way through college."

Parents Contribution. Need help paying for college? Here's one answer: ask your parents for money.

Other. This is one of those words like "misc." that says nothing except "this will help make the balance sheet balance." For all you know, it could mean "go rob a bank to make up the difference."

Estimated Expenses	*Sources of Income*
	Parents Contribution: $ 2000
	You & your hard-earned
Tuition: $ 3528	summer dollars: 2000
Room: 1219	*Aid Needed*
Board: 1874	
Books: 300	
Travel: 900	Loan: 2100
Personal: 500	Grant: 50
	Self-Help: 2000
	Other: 171
Total: Lots of Money	
	Total: Lots of money

The Austere Life

Not even Franciscan monks can live on a personal allowance of $500 a year. This figure breaks down to:

$500 divided by 28 school weeks at $ 17.50 a week, which will get you plenty, if you're wise and frugal and don't spend it recklessly as non-college goers might. For example,

$ 0.39 worth of toothpaste for the week
  0.12 soap
  0.15 shaving cream
  0.89 razor blades
  0.78 shampoo
  0.34 underarm deodorant
  1.75 very personal items
  0.75 other personal
  1.20 stamps
  0.90 stationery
  0.15 ink for pen
  5.34 depreciation on clothing
  0.55   "   " sheets, blankets
  0.95   "   " lamps, posters, desk aids, plant
  1.50 *Time* or *Cosmo* magazine
  0.35 candy bar (you deserve to splurge a little at the end of a hard week of saving.)
  1.50 weekend flicks

And the total of $17.50 adds up to a good, solid college education and the makings of a thrifty American citizen. Few problems, though.

You won't be able to afford:

a) any sports events off-campus
b) off-campus dining
c) going out with friends
d) music
e) gifts
f) investing in real estate

Cutting Corners

There are many ways to survive and even thrive while on financial aid. The key is in spending less on some of the assigned values (such as travel, books, and board) while spending more on others (such as personal, misc., personal, room, and personal). Keep in mind that a student on financial aid who seeks no outside help is usually unable to lead a normal social life and sometimes turns into an underachiever or a civil servant. Don't let this happen to you.

Travel. Two round-trip flights, one at Christmas and the other for summer, is about all you'll be able to afford with a $900 allowance if you've chosen a school far from home. You can "save" this money in many ways.

1) *Thumbing:* saves lots, but takes time. You may not have the patience for this.
2) *Driving:* borrow a friend's car; tell him you need to do a few errands, and that you'll be right back; drive home; enjoy vacation. There will be more friends in college, so don't let the after effects of this money saver bother you.
3) *UPS yourself* (remember to put air holes in box).
4) *Hold on to railroad undercarriage.*
5) *Build and fly own aircraft.*

Books. Your book costs will depend mostly on your major. If you're a history or philosophy major, count on spending a lot more than science majors. Listed below are ways of obtaining books, beginning with the most expensive methods and progressing to the most economical.

1) *The campus bookstore* is a great place to shop.
2) *Used bookstores* will give you great discounts.
3) *Look for upperclassmen* who have taken the same introductory courses as you are now planning; offer to buy their books.
4) *See if your roommate* is taking the same courses; some large textbooks tend to be very expensive and easy to share.
5) *Check the books out* of the library; a two week or permanent solution, depending on the way you check out the books.
6) *Don't do the reading.*

EIGHT

OVER THERE

SPENDING TIME IN EUROPE

Spending a year abroad has become a natural part of the college career for many students. Generally, the college student decides to go overseas only after realizing that the possibilities for study abroad exist. Sometimes these opportunities entice would-be freshmen to enroll at college. Other times a sophomore's parents will encourage him or her to apply for the overseas program and take the giant leap. In any case, few students regret the year spent away from home.

A vast majority of these students venture to Europe, and quite naturally, for Europe represents the birth of Western Civilization, the ancestral home of many Americans, and the only place left where you can still buy a pizza for less then five bucks. If you want to get away from American college life for a while, but you're not up for learning Swahili, Europe's the place to go.

Virtually any experience in Europe is an educational one. Strolling through Amsterdam or touring Madrid is certainly more educational than another day in Smith Hall. Those first two years in school were hard work, and it's about time you got a chance to relax. Why should you sit in a hot classroom stuggling through Ancient Cultures 101, when you could be taking in some real Greek culture while lying on a sunny beach.

Meeting Europeans

When you step out of the plane in Rome, you'll see many Italians, most of them Romans. You'll notice that Italians look like what you've always thought Italians would look like. You'll find yourself stereotyping nationalities wherever you go. Whenever you see a German drinking beer out of a huge stein or a Parisian carrying a loaf of bread long enough to play hockey with, your inclination to stereoptype will increase to the point where you'll feel cheated if you don't see any Dutch wearing wooden shoes. Before you get to Europe, learn a little about the people who live there.

---

1) **Europe is not America.** After identifying a few familiar Americanisms, many American travelers make the mistake of thinking they're right at home and get carried away. So while you're munching on a Big Mac in Vienna, remember you're still a guest and that when in Austria, do as the Austrians do.

2) **Europeans like Americans.** Although some political types will remind you of one of the American government's latest gaffes, and someone will eventually bring up Vietnam, most Europeans do admire Americans . . . even the French.

3) **Not all Europeans speak English,** though many do. Try to speak the language of whatever country you're visiting no matter how little you know. You'll flatter the people immensely, and you'll never really have to communicate in that language because an English-speaking local will eventually step in. If you're in Europe to improve your Spanish or Norwegian or whatever, you'll find it extra frustrating when the locals insist on practicing their rudimentary English on YOU. If you want to be polite but firm, keep responding in the vernacular no matter what they say. If you want to be rude, slap them in the face and remind them how much you paid for your plane ticket.

4) **Europeans are often sharper** politically, culturally, and linguistically than Americans. Unlike America and neighbors, European nations live in close quarters; consequently they learn each others' languages and become aware of cultural differences from an early age. Even with their great culture, they still don't have Frosted Mini-Wheats.

5) **Europeans can be obnoxious.** You can be more obnoxious. It's easy; you're an American.

6) **European males are frequently attracted** to American females. Just as you've always heard, southern European young men fantasize about picking up American girls. Somehow, these men have heard stories about how "easy" American women are. Strangely, many American men haven't.

Eurail Syndrome

While still in America, most overseas-bound students will be curious about how to travel around. Soon they discover that, unlike North America, Europe features an excellent railroad network and the only decision the student has to make is what train tickets to buy. Soon students discover that train passes are probably much cheaper and more convenient for their needs. A Eurail pass costs a little over $ 300.00 and is good for any eight weeks you choose. An Interrail pass costs around $200.00and, though only good for four weeks, includes the United Kingdom and Eastern Europe. For the advantages of these rail passes, we highly recommend buying your own copy of *Let's Go: Europe*. Look out for the one drawback with using these passes.

Every year thousands of Americans in Europe are struck by a vicious, merciless disease. Wary of Italian water, French chicken, and German sausage, these same Americans later discover that they've been distracted by false alarms only to have fallen victim to the real European killer: **Eurail Syndrome.**

The symptoms:
- Waking up in the middle of the night to ask, *"What country are we in?"*
Showing your passport to every uniformed official
Living on bread, cheese and water (even train water)
Map growth off right hand
Look of uncertainty

Where victims can be spotted:
- Train station, especially near time schedules and cheap hotels close by
Overnight (over-weekend) trains to
Barcelona
Being crushed by backpacks in train vestibules

Duration of disease:
- eight weeks (Interail Syndrome lasts only four weeks)

Administer for recovery:
- real food
non-moving beds
hot showers
identities

Euroscam

After working hard in the coal mines all summer and after milking your parents for a grand, you can finally buy the gear, plane ticket, and Eurail necessary for the big trip to Europe. Once you arrive in Europe you'll realize the last thing you want to do is spend your hard-earned cash on a subway ticket in Paris. You've got to save that fifty cents for more important things like a crepe or some postcards. All in all, you'll discover you can save hundreds of lira, francs, pounds, or marks by mastering the euroscams and cheating (a little) on public transportation.

Subways. With very little effort, you can save a bundle of cash by scamming on the subways of Europe. Security systems are usually weak or nonexistent, and conductors are few and far between. The only catch is applying the proper method in each country.
Germany: usually no authorities on board. If you get caught, use the "I forgot to buy a ticket" plea.
France: usually no authorities in stations. Use the "jump the turnstiles" method.
England: usually authorities everywhere. Use the "I don't want to end up like the guy in *Midnight Express*" plan.

Buses. It's a bit harder to scam on buses than it is on subways, but in some countries, Italy for instance, a bus ride can become a free ride. It is a dilemma; Italian bus rides usually cost between fifteen and twenty-five cents, so you've got to decide if your conscience is worth a quarter.

Trains. You'll find it extremely difficult to use the Euroscam method on international trains. Aggressive conductors and suspicious police will usually quash any subversive plans you might have. Instead, scam wildly on local trains. If there's no conductor, you ride for free. If there is an authority on board, hide in the bathroom or get off the train before he gets to your compartment. Remember, they're on the honor system. They're also naive.

Planes. Try hijacking. If you plan really well, obtain a great lawyer, and get a couple of lucky breaks, you might be able to avoid the death penalty.

Hostels:
A Grubby Europe

Making a king's tour of Europe while on a pauper's wages necessitates some compromises. The Youth Hostel is meant to facilitate these compromises by providing cheap lodging for groups of youths who are undergoing the same experiences. Hostels can be a places to meet students from all countries and walks of life in settings which range from modern and beautiful in Innsbruck to grungy and barrackslike in Venice. You'll want to know what to expect when you check into them.

1) **Toilets.** Most hostels have these, though some may be outside, and others in weird shapes. They're all there for the same purpose, so don't be intimidated.

2) **Check out time.** Make sure you know ahead of time when you'll need to check out in the morning. In most cases, you'll have until 10 or 11 o'clock; if not, be prepared for a rude awakening by either loud disco music or loud foreigners.

3) **Linen.** This is the most difficult aspect of hostels for Americans to understand. Hostel management won't let you use your brand-new $200 sleeping bag, but you can use a couple of dirty sheets sewn together (which they'll graciously sell you.)

4) **Food.** Meals are served at some hostels. They are usually very cheap and range from a bowl of coffee and a roll to a roll and a bowl of coffee. Some places even offer coffee and rolls.

5) **Cooking facilities.** If a hostel has these, you're in business. You can buy food and cook it right there, often while having a good conversation with a foreigner. The facilities are not extensive, but if you like grilled cheese sandwiches then they're fine.

6) **Location.** Some hostels are right downtown within walking distance of ancient historical sites. Others are miles from the city and are ancient historical sites in themselves.

If you go Europe, you will be told a million times, "don't overpack." Don't overpack. You'll want to travel lightly in a foreign country since you'll want to avoid any extra hassles. Take

Over

the bare essentials, plus a couple of luxury items to make

What to Bring

2 pairs jeans
1 pair khakis
Coat
5 pair underwear
1 pair tennis shoes
5 pair socks
Swiss army knife
Traveler's checks
Money belt
Backpack
Let's Go: Europe
Europe on $15 a Day
Hotel New Hampshire
How to See Europe Cheaply
How Not to Get Cheated
*   in Europe*
Camera & 2 rolls of film
Key to the front door
   of house
Adapter
Travel alarm
Personal hygienics

1 pair jeans	Traveler's checks	Latest copy of *Glamour*
2 pair khakis	Purse	*Europe on $15 a Day*
1 skirt	Pair of Nike's	Travel alarm
5 pair socks	Backpack	Camera & 10 rolls of film
3 blouses	2 pair shoes	Personal hygenics
1 sweater	*Let's Go: Europe*	

and Back

your stay a little easier. As for returning to America,

you'll inevitably have more to bring back. Don't be alarmed. With everything you've lost, there will be plenty of room for your European purchases.

What To Bring Back

1 pair jeans
1 pair underwear
1 pair socks
$2.67
Guide to the Louvre
Guide to the Uffizi
Guide to the Parthenon
Map of Rome
Map of London
Map of Paris
Posters
Expired Eurail Pass
Stolen beer mug and coasters
  from the Hofbrau House
Several old bus tickets
Shredded copy of
  Let's Go: Europe
Journal
Letters from parents
  and friends
Ticket stubs from plays
Foreign coins
European haircut

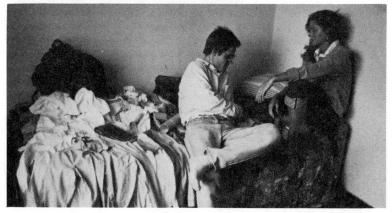

Laura Ashley dresses	5 pair socks	Diary
Posters	5 blouses	Foreign goods
Great pics taken from all over	2 dresses	Leather goods
Perfumes	1 alpine hat	Personal hygienics
Pen pals	Chocolate	*Savoir Faire*
5 pair underwear	Matches from every restaurant	Boyfriend

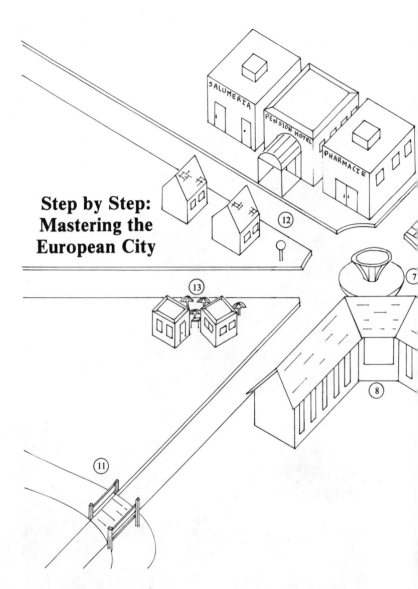

Step by Step: Mastering the European City

1) Get off train. Scan headlines at newsstand.

2) Scrutinize train schedule for departure time.

3) Check in backpack.

4) Pick up brochures for yacht rides and expensive hotels at information booth.

5) Use restrooms (for showering, shaving, brushing teeth, etc.).

6) Catch Bus 13B to the Place Republique, Piazza Republica, or Stadtplatz (Town Square).

7) Ask a "local" to take a picture of you in front of the fountain. Immediately discover that the "local" is John Q. Public from Oakville, Ohio.

8) Wander aimlessly through famous 17th century art museum.

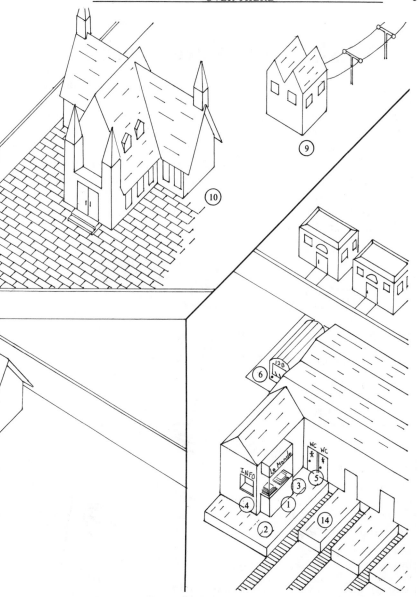

9) Fork over a dollar or more to ride elevator to top of tower, to climb stairs of bell tower, or to cruise in aerial tram.

10) Be astounded by beauty and structure of cathedral.

11) Savor bread and cheese along river bank.

12) Stroll along main boulevard and reminisce about sophomore year.

13) Splurge for hot cocoa at sidewalk cafe. Peruse *International Herald Tribune* or *Time* magazine. Notice how late it's getting.

14) Exciting city: run and leap to catch moving train (as in movies). Boring city: sit around train station an hour early waiting for train.

Wish You Were Here

While you'll be over in Europe having the time of your life, many of your friends will still be back home at school working hard. In a way, you'll feel sorry for them because they'll actually have to study to earn units; imagine studying six hours a day in the library just to get the same credit as eating *pain* and *fromage* on the banks of the river Siene?

Send postcards to your friends back home to let them know you're having the time of your life. And don't let them forget it; send a postcards each week . . . from a different European city each time.

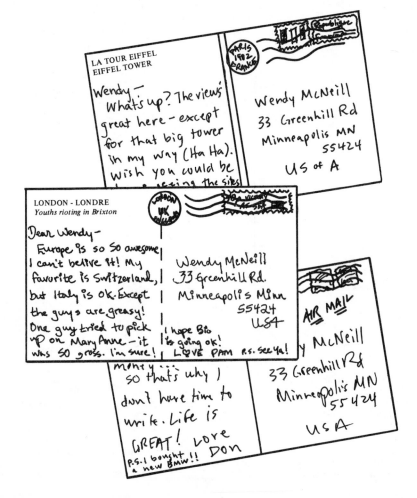

An American in Paris

Many Europeans haughtily remark that from a mile away, they can spot an American walking through the streets of their home city. To verify their claims, try to spot the American out of the crowd below. (Hint: the American is not wearing Eau de Cologne aftershave.)

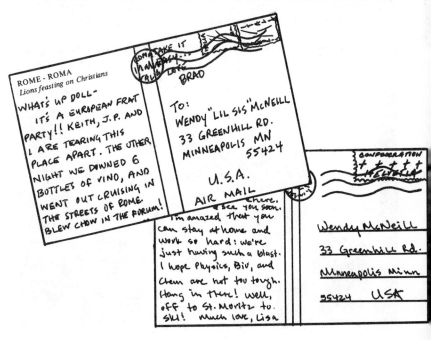

ROME - ROMA
Lions feasting on Christians

WHAT'S UP DOLL-
IT'S A EUROPEAN FRAT
PARTY!! KEITH, J.P. AND
I ARE TEARING THIS
PLACE APART. THE OTHER
NIGHT WE DOWNED 6
BOTTLES OF VINO, AND
WENT OUT CRUISING IN
THE STREETS OF ROME.
BLEW CHOW IN THE FORUM!

ROMA TAKE IT
IT'S AN EASY...
CALL ME LATER
BRAD

TO:
WENDY "LIL SIS" McNEILL
33 GREENHILL RD.
MINNEAPOLIS MN
55424

U.S.A.

AIR MAIL

there.
See you soon.

I'm amazed that you
can stay at home and
work so hard: we're
just having such a blast.
I hope Physics, Bio, and
Chem are not too tough.
Hang in there! Well,
off to St. Moritz to
ski! Much love, Lisa

CONFEDERATION
HELVETICA

Wendy McNeill
33 Greenhill Rd.
Minneapolis Minn
55424 USA

Showing Off

When the dust has finally settled and you've recovered from your dose of culture shock, you'll want to show your slides to all your friends and family. With pride you'll point out every statue, plaza, museum, and ice cream parlor in Europe. Just as in the postcards, you'll want everyone to know that you had the time of your life and that you can't wait to go back.

You may want to present an elaborate slide show. With transparencies arranged in perfect order to give the audience a "walking tour of London," you can put on Mozart's Fourth for background effect and use a long pointer to highlight some of the fine points of European culture. Or you may decide that passing around a few dozen copies of friend's prints will suffice. Or you may keep their presentations even shorter. "Europe? Yeah, it was fun."

By the end of the evening, you'll inevitably notice that everyone is dozing off, except for your friends that have already been overseas. At first, they'll just toss out a few questions like "Did you ever eat at that *pastisserie* on the Champs Elysees?" but in no time you'll both be exchanging stories and reminiscing like fiends. Later you'll notice that everyone else is actually sleeping.

NINE

THE
LAST
ACT

SENIOR YEAR

For twenty two years, you've always known what you were going to do next. You always had a plan, or at least your parents had one for you. Now, as you stand on the diving board of senior year, ready to jump into the pool of life, you pray that you don't do a belly flop. Don't worry. You won't. But you're going to have to go through the bittersweet experience of senior year just like everyone else.

Ideally, senior year should be icing on the cake of college. You should do a little interviewing, a little applying to graduate schools, a little studying, and a lot of partying. Unfortunately, things don't always work out that way.

Most students forget that they actually have to do work senior year. You may study during the first semester, but as the year comes to an end and you have so much else that you want to do, it's hard to continue to put an emphasis on school. What senior cares about subjects like Dostoevsky's view of religion? You just need the units to get out of the place.

Senior year is the time for reflection on your academic career. You may begin to think that you picked the wrong major, or that you did not take advantages of all of your opportunities. Don't worry about it. Have a beer.

If you decide to apply to grad schools you'll find out that the admissions tests are neither inexpensive nor fun. If you somehow avoid the pressure to take one of those expensive preparatory classes (which you'll blow off half the time anyway), then you're in for some fun with one of the preparatory books (which you'll also blow off). Of course, you don't have to prepare. Though you'll worry more about the grad school tests than you did for the SAT, you'll probably end up studying less.

Once you've applied to some grad schools, you'll probably want to look for a job just in case you get rejected or change your mind. This involves going to the Career Placement center and signing up for some interviews. Some students only last through one or two interviews. They usually end up forgetting the whole thing and going home for a while to sort things out. Other students are persistent and get good jobs. They usually end up rubbing their starting salary figure in the face of the others.

Even if you get a job, it's only natural to be depressed over leaving college, especially since alumni keep telling you that college is the best time of your life. The end of college means the end of the best friendships you've ever had, the end of a diligent pursuit of knowledge for knowledges's sake, and the end of free beer on Friday night. These are not things to be taken lightly. If you had a choice, would you trade the free interplay of ideas, sex, and good times of college for the expensive parking, bad plumbing, and high pressure of a job in Baltimore?

Some of the fondest memories of college are made in the last few months, but most seniors come out of their final year more or less ready to move on to something new. It takes senior year for you to realize that, yes, there IS life after college, although that life may be very different than what you had expected four years before.

To Each another College

After four long, and often enjoyable, years within the walls of academia, most students are happy to be finally finishing, if only to join the end of the unemployment line. Some students will elect to continue their higher education by getting even higher. The choice of where to go next has become smaller, as the application process to grad schools is very unlike the wide open process of selecting an undergraduate liberal arts school. Students interested in pursuing higher degrees know this and often plan their undergraduate careers around applying to grad schools.

Law School. Despite the glut of lawyers on the market, law school remains the most popular choice of a continuing academic career among liberal arts majors. The only explanation for wanting to go to law school is a desire to seek justice, prepare for a Capitol Hill career, and to be as cool as Timothy Bottoms in *The Paper Chase*.

Business School. Although it's nearly impossible to get into a great biz school, it's easy getting into an average school. The reasons behind going: to seek profits, prepare for a capitalistic career, and to be as rich as J.R. in *Dallas*.

Med Schools. After four years of hard work and thousands and thousands of dollars spent, med school finally pays off: you can pick up free surgeon's clothes.

Schools of Education. If you really enjoyed the last 18 years of school (including pre-school), maybe you'll want to spend the rest of your life there.

Schools of Engineering. For the liberal arts major who wants to learn how to drive a train.

The GPA

Historically, the GPA has loomed, plotted, and destroyed. With his chief political opponent out of the way and all of Rome urging him on, Brutus was ecstatic and optimistic. But he hadn't counted on that last semester at Forum University being so darn challenging, and he ultimately broke down upon receiving his fifteenth and final letter of rejection from law schools. As he hurled himself in despair from the top of the Leaning Tower of Pisa, Brutus was last heard uttering from his grief-stricken voice, "Et tu, GPA?"

(Incidentally, Brutus fell at the very same moment as did Cicero, who weighed three times as much. When they simultaneously hit the pavement, nearby Galileo scribbled furiously into his notebook. He got into law school.)

The Job Interviewing Scene

School's been fun. In fact, school's been great. Yet one morning you'll wake up and realize that it won't last forever. At first you'll panic and wonder where your friends will go, where you'll be able to kick back, eat Haagen-Daz double dip, and wear T-shirts and jeans to your heart's content. Eventually you realize that these are the least of your troubles and of course you'll be able to do all of these with even more freedom once you get out of school.

First, you've got to get a job. Getting a job is a job in itself, so you'll have to understand and eventually master the job hunting scene.

THE CAREER CENTER

Your school, no doubt, will have a Career Placement and Planning Center (CPPC). If it doesn't, it probably has a PPCC (Placement and Planning Center for Careers), or possibly a PCPC (Planning Careers and Placement Center), but not a CCCP (Soviet Union). There are several ways of using the Center's resources to help you secure a job:

1) Start sweating it in September of your senior year; register with the Center immediately; aggressively pursue major multinational corporations. **Right Way!**

2) Just after the graduation ceremony, stroll over in your cap and gown and ask if there are any openings for a $22,000/year job. **Wrong Way!**

The problem most students encounter with their Centers is that they are intimidated by the hoard of "high-pressure" brochures, the arrogance of ubiquitous three-piece suits, and the columns of sign-up lists. Try to "wade into the water" slowly rather than dive in head first. Only after frequenting the Center several times will you begin to become familiar with the procedures, more comfortable with the ambience, and more confident in your job hunting. You'll still detest the brochures, the ubiquitous three piece suits, and the columns of sign-up lists.

Liberal Arts

If you're a Liberal Arts student, you'll begin to feel the competition immediately.

> *"Hi, I'm thinking about getting a job and I'd like to register."*
> *"Fine! Fabulous! Fantastic! I'm sure you'll find the Center quite helpful in your search for a first job. Before we can go any further, we have to know whether you're in Engineering or Liberal Arts."*
> *"Liberal Arts."*
> *"Oh. Can you cut grass?"*

After a little exploring of the Center, you'll realize that they were indeed telling the truth about having a lot of facilities, but you won't really care. To you, the bottom line will be, are they going to help you get a job?

Reading the newspaper every day will keep you up to date on the job scene. You'll know when opportunity knocks, but will you be able to open the door in time? Push often come to shove in the job center, especially when the very prestigious investment banking firms arrive. Every school has a different sign-up procedure and the real trick is to master the system.

STANLEY F. KINGSTON

School	Home
39 Campus Drive	220 Argus Court
Wichita, KS 67276	Wichita, KS 67276
(316) 333-1982	(316) 878-3546

OBJECTIVE: To obtain a position as a junior executive in a top-level investment banking firm, making use of my natural leadership skills and dynamic thought process.

EDUCATION:

9/78-6/82   *Wichita State University,* Wichita, Kansas
Degree in Business Administration. Undergraduate coursework includes extensive studies in management, business communication, accounting, business today, business and you, history of business, young businessmen in the 20th century (A+ in this course), investment analysis, post-business careers (dropped this course), God and business, gods of business, lacrosse.

9/74-6/78   *East Wichita High School,* Wichita, Kansas
Student body treasurer; President, Future Business Leaders of America; 4.0 GPA in Pre-Business Curriculum; Lacrosse Team.

WORK EXPERIENCE:

9/81-6/82   *Treasurer,* Wichita State Business Association, Wichita, Kansas. Responsible for accounting and allocation of pecuniary interests for large scale campus group.

9/80-6/81   *Literary Material Supervisor,* Wichita State University Business Library, Wichita, Kansas. Supervised handling and distribution of literary material. Duties included inspection of literary contraband and authority to approve removal of material.

Summers   *Sales Marketing Representative,* McDonald's, Wichita, Kansas. Managed sales of consumer merchandise for major firm (Gross income 1982 $1.3 billion). Supervised removal of waste hindering production at the strategic operational level.

9/72-6/73   *Major Media Distribution Executive,* Wichita Herald Tribune, Wichita, Kansas. Supervised, collected, collated, distributed major media product to consumers. Provided vital communications link between important news events and households.

ADDITIONAL INFORMATION:

Lacrosse Club; Member of Wichita State Business Association; Lead in "How to Succeed In Business"; Hobbies include: following stock market, reading Wall Street Journal, and Lacrosse.

REFERENCES:

Available on request at Career Placement Center, 39 Campus Drive, Wichita, Kansas.

JOHN E. MILLER

P.O. Box 1020
Columbus, OH 43216
(614) 291-1304

121 Main Street
Columbus, OH 43216
(614) 923-3497

OBJECTIVE: To get a job.

EDUCATION:

Ohio State University, Columbus, Ohio. B.A. degree in Economics. Some coursework in history, math, and sociology.

WORK EXPERIENCE:

Staff Member, Ohio State Library System. Checked out and shelved books.

Worker, McDonald's, Columbus, Ohio. Sold hamburgers, wiped tables, mopped floor and took out trash for fast food store.

Paperboy, Columbus Times, Columbus, Ohio. Delivered papers to people's houses.

ADDITIONAL INFORMATION:

IM football, junior year;
Bit part in dorm play, sophomore year.

REFERENCES:

Available upon request.

Your First Interview

The key word here is preparation. Appearance and familiarity with the interviewing company will ensure you the job you've always wanted and every publication on job seeking will tell you this. You've got to be in better position than all the other applicants; you'll want a few tips.

Most people realize that going into an interview with potato salad breath could hurt their chances, but did YOU know that wearing shoes the color of cantelope could ruin your chances if your interviewer were a Libra? Probably not, that's why you'll want to read on in preparation for your first interview.

A Few Types Of Sign-Up Procedures

The Bidding System. The students are allotted a certain number of bid points at the beginning of the academic year. They use these points to "bid" for the interview spots. Highest bidders are allowed to sign up for the interviews.

The Open Sign-Up Sheet. Commonly called the "first come, first serve" system, this method is based on providing sign up sheets to anyone who is willing to make sure he or she is in line first. The inevitable happens: the red hots win the day by getting in line before dawn.

The Resume System. This system is found at many small schools with no Center. Students send their resumes to appealing firms and hope that they are offered an interview.

The Hat System. The names of interested students are put into two black top hats: one for Engineering, the other for Liberal Arts. Everyone who submitted a resume stands by while the company interviewers draw names.

Dress to Impress

Dress depends entirely on the type of job you'll be interviewing for. The key to any interview dressing game is to "look the part," so you'll want to dress exactly as you would on the job. For those of you interviewing for sales jobs, dress varies widely. Many hopefuls will feel the J.P. Morgan Look is just what they need

Selling computers. Don't go so far as to walk in carrying file paper under one arm and a keyboard-patterned tie with a terminal tie clasp; keep in mind that Pascal is a computer language, not a fashion designer.

Selling Sony Walkmans. Show your appreciation and knowledge of the product. Wear one to the interview. Pretend not to notice someone's speaking to you. Nod head to beat. Answer at twice the decibels. Remove headset and ask him to repeat the question.

Teaching. This very competitive occupation (due to its glut of applicants) requires an extra effort. Using the "dress as you would" guideline, carefully analyze the teaching post.

Prep School: old, worn-out sweater, khaki pants, button-down candy striped shirt, and Topsiders or Hush Puppies.
Gym Teacher: warmups, T-shirt from college, smelly B-ball shoes, kickball, and whistle.
Elementary School: overalls, plaid shirt, and saddle shoes.
University Prof: polyester flood pants, short sleeve shirt, sandals, and scraggly beard.

Peace Corps (the altruistic look): jeans, flannel shirt, backpack, and two years of your life.

Engineering: anything.

The J.P. Morgan Look-Alike

Prospective career candidates should dress as they suppose J.P. himself would have. Generally, those who have done the most research on how J.P. actually dressed are also the most successful interviewees.

The conservative look has made considerable gains in the last decade over most other types of dress. Special attention must be given to every detail of dress. Colors often lack flair, and many applicants opt for white (which shows good moral fiber), gray (which shows lack of tackiness), or blue (which shows aversion to white and gray). Clothing should be carefully pressed and shoes of the finest leather highly polished. You'll want to overwhelm your interviewer with professionalism.

Don your one and only business suit, slip into your best shoes, and hope like hell you don't sit on a Fudgsicle.

The conservative look is the staple of:

Investment bankers
Commercial bankers
Financial consultants
Stockbrokers
Accountants
Management executives
Insurance salesmen
Drug dealers

Some Interviewing Don't's

If you're really worried about interviews, you've probably picked up every booklet, manual, handbook, and primer on the subject. All of these will confidently tell you how to act during the interview and many will suggest what to say. None, unfortunately, inform you about what NOT to say.

"Hi, I'm Helene. I'm the chick your company's lookin' for."

"Hey!! Bob's the name, interviewing's my game! Mind if I call you "Fatso"? I hate being stuffy and formal. That's why I wore these Bermuda shorts."

"Nine o'clock is kind of early. Could I come to work a half hour later? To tell the truth, Mr. Moore, I'm slow and groggy in the morning and I don't get rolling until around noon or so"

"How big will my office be? Do you think I could fit a double bed in it?"

"Hmmmm. Well, that's not very much, and with my hobbies, I'm not sure I could get by on that little."

"Could you please stop drooling, Mrs. Everson. It's really grossing me out."

"Belllcccccchhhhhhh."

"Some friends of mine told me that the firm whips their management trainees like slaves. Is that true?"

"Look, are you finished yet? I told my boyfriend I'd meet him outside the quad right now and . . . "

"Think I got a good shot at the job? I've seen some of the others in here, and they look like losers!"

Wanted: A Future

Around graduation time, the Want Ads in the school paper often brim with offers for lucrative and fulfilling employment.

ENGINEERS !!!!

Interested in the exciting field of plastic lids? We at LIDCO can offer you a secure future. Cover up those job worries and join the gang at LIDCO!

SOFT DRINK LIDS! GARBAGE CAN LIDS! MEDICINE BOTTLE LIDS!

LIDCO - Makers of lids for over three years.

JOIN THE TEAM !!!

AT GENERAL CONFUSION

If you're an EE, IE, ME, or EI-EI-O, you may be just the person we need on our team at General Confusion.

At General Confusion we make very tiny particles that do billions of things though they are the size of bacteria. We're dedicated to making those particles smaller and smaller, and we want you to help us. Come and be confused with us.

GENERAL CONFUSION:

Makers of very small, intricate, highly sensitive things.

LIBERAL ARTS MAJORS

Who says all those papers you wrote were for naught? We at

KELLEY GIRL
Secretarial Services

are looking for bright people like yourself - someone who can type, file, collate, and staple.

Don't be ashamed!
Sign up at Kelley Girl.

The Finishing Touches

It's almost over. You've gone through four years of academics, extra-curricular activities, and social situations. You've survived the tough classes, the losing football games, and the bad parties. You may have gone to Europe, and you've probably even planned a future of some sort. But that's all in the past; now it's time to move on.

NOT SO FAST. One thing still remains: graduation. Before you dash off to enroll in graduate school, to work in a large, comfortable office, or to join the Lebanese army, you have to go through all the pomp and circumstance that surrounds graduation from college.

Graduation may seem a little rigid and formal, but what the hell. For once, be rigid and formal. It's a big moment, so your best bet is to relax and enjoy the ceremony: besides, you've earned the right to enjoy it.

Don't relax for too long. You've got to get dressed for the boring cocktail party afterward where you'll entertain people with stories from your undergraduate days.

College Graduates	NOT College Graduates
Mike Smith	Jack Smith
Mary Smith	Betty Smith
Harvey Smith	Bob Smith
Susan Smith	Carol Smith
Jared Smith	Ted Smith
Jeanne Smith	Alice Smith
American Airlines	Braniff Airlines
England	Argentina
God	The Devil

It's Over

Match these traditional aspects of graduation with the comments below.

1. Renting your cap and gown.
2. Drinking champagne.
3. Receiving your diploma.
4. Taking pictures.
5. Spending time with parents and relatives.
6. Listening to speeches by prominent people.
7. Waiting for final grades.
8. Partying all night.

a. *"Thanks. But this is only a piece of paper."*

b. *"You look so great. I can't believe you're graduating already. It seems like only yesterday that you were knee high to a grasshopper."*

c. *"And as you go forth today, from these hallowed groves of knowledge and enlightenment to a world torn by strife and depression, you must remember that your generation will be the one with a chance to change the world. You are in a very precarious, yet envious situation."*

d. *"I never drink. But this is graduation, and a lot of people drink to celebrate. I guess it is traditional. Okay, pass the bubbly."*

e. *"Here, let's get one with Kari and Mike. No, how about Kari, Mike, and Robby. Okay, everybody smile. Quit hamming it up, Robby. Ready? Oh, damn. There's no film in here."*

f. *"Please, God, I hope I passed Psych. Just let me have passed."*

g. *"What size do I need? I hate these things. They make me look like a judge or a priest."*

h. *"Arghhhhhh!"*

Answers: 1g; 2d; 3a; 4e; 5b; 6c; 7f; 8h.